Eyewitness Accounts of the American Revolution

The Siege of Penobscot
Edited by John Calef

The New York Times & Arno Press

Reprint Edition 1971 by Arno Press Inc.

*

LC# 78-140857
ISBN 0-405-01226-8

*

Eyewitness Accounts of the American Revolution, Series III
ISBN for complete set: 0-405-01187-3

*

Manufactured in the United States of America

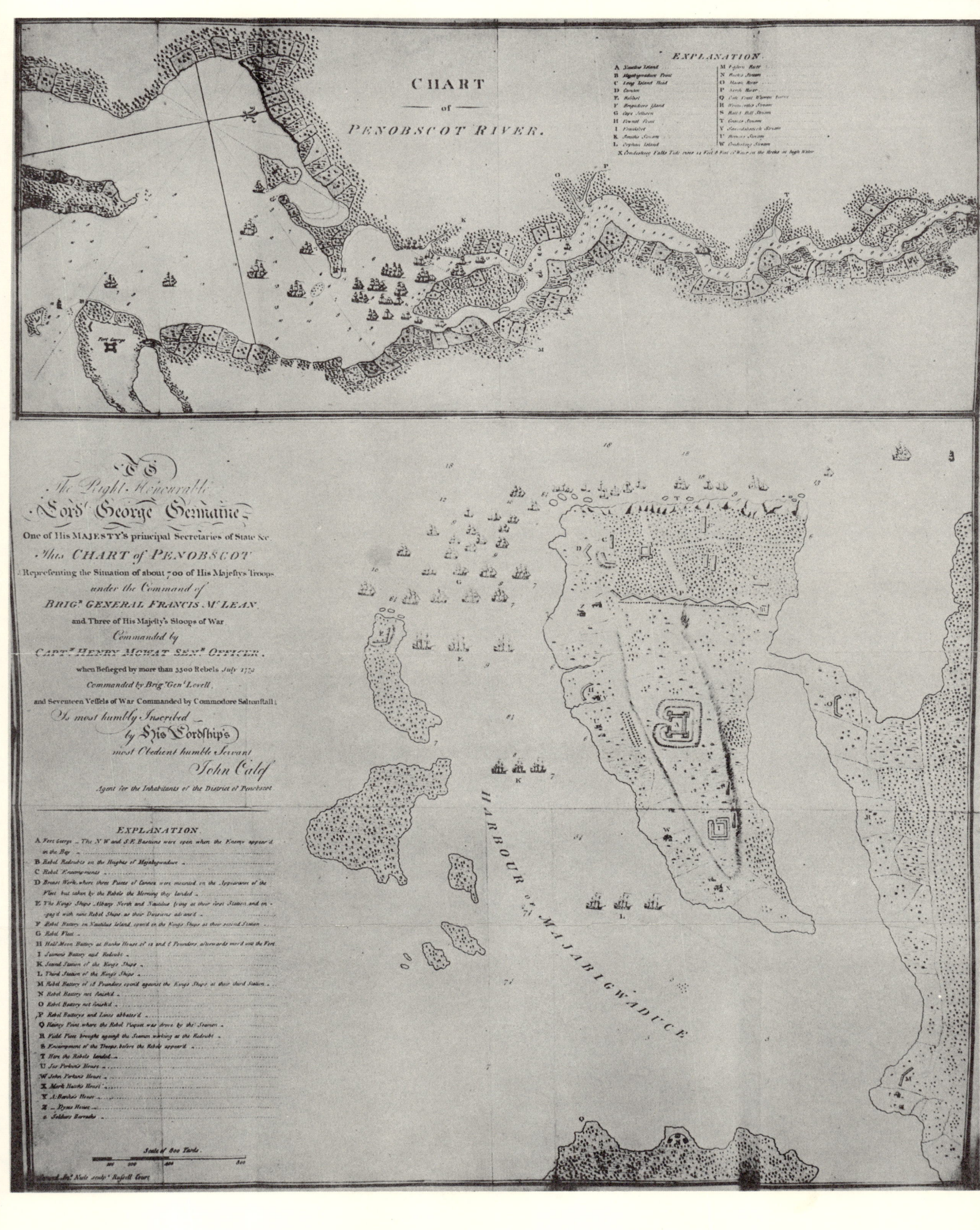

*This reproduction of the original map
in the Lenox Library, New York,
is about one-quarter size.*

As near a facsimile of the original as possible.

THE
SIEGE OF *PENOBSCOT*
BY THE
REBELS;

CONTAINING A

JOURNAL of the PROCEEDINGS

OF

His MAJESTY's FORCES detached from the 74th and 82d REGIMENTS, confifting of about 700 Rank and File, under the Command of Brigadier-General FRANCIS M'LEAN,

AND OF

THREE of His MAJESTY's SLOOPS of WAR, of 16 Guns each, under the Command of Captain HENRY MOWAT, Senior Officer;

WHEN BESIEGED BY

THREE THOUSAND THREE HUNDRED (Rebel) Land Forces, under the Command of Brigadier-General *Solomon Lovell*,

AND

SEVENTEEN Rebel Ships and Veffels of War, under the Command of *G. Saltonftall*, Commodore.

TO WHICH IS ANNEXED

A PROCLAMATION iffued June 15, 1779, by General M'LEAN and Captain BARCLAY to the Inhabitants;

ALSO

Brigadier-General *Lovell's* PROCLAMATION to the Inhabitants; and his LETTER to Commodore *Saltonftall*, found on board the Rebel Ship *Hunter*;

TOGETHER WITH

The Names, Force, and Commanders, of the Rebel Ships deftroyed in PENOBSCOT BAY and RIVER, *Auguft* 14 and 15, 1779.

WITH

A CHART of the Peninfula of MAJABIGWADUCE, and of PENOBSCOT River.

TO WHICH IS SUBJOINED

A POSTSCRIPT, wherein a fhort Account of the Country of PENOBSCOT is given.

By *J. C.* Efq. a Volunteer.

LONDON:
Printed for G. KEARSLEY, in *Fleet-Street*, and ASHBY and NEELE, (late SPILSBURY's) in *Ruffel-Court*, *Covent-Garden*.
M,DCC,LXXXI.

NEW YORK
Reprinted
WILLIAM ABBATT
1910

(Being Extra No. 11 of THE MAGAZINE OF HISTORY WITH NOTES AND QUERIES.)

THE
SIEGE OF *PENOBSCOT;*

CONTAINING A

JOURNAL OF THE PROCEEDINGS

OF

His Majesty's Forces againſt the Rebels in *July*, 1779:

AND

A POSTSCRIPT, giving ſome Account of the Country,
&c. &c.

EDITOR'S PREFACE

THE "Siege of Penobscot," so called, was the attempt of the Colony of Massachusetts Bay to dislodge the British from the peninsula of Majabagaduce,* where the present town of Castine, Maine, now is, a most historic locality. The British landed June 17, 1779, and began work toward the building of a fort which, at first, was called Fort Castine and later Fort George, for the King.

It had been decided to establish there a military post where ships could bring their prizes and where the Loyalists of New England could have a place of refuge. The Loyalists availed themselves of this privilege until the place became a considerable village. The British idea was that if the Colonists secured their independence the boundary line between the United States and Canada would not be east of the Penobscot, and in that event they would have a fort already built, at the head of Penobscot Bay, in a very advantageous situation. The territory between the Penobscot and St. Croix rivers would become a new province, of which Castine would be the capital.

The attempt to dislodge the British by the Massachusetts Bay Colony was the largest of our Revolutionary naval undertakings, but was a deplorable failure. It is said to have cost the Colony £1,739,174: 11.4 d. when their finances were at a very low ebb. The Americans were seized with a panic, their ships destroyed and the people were disheartened. The cause of the failure was the conduct of Saltonstall, the commander of the fleet, and the unpreparedness of the expedition. The land forces were hastily

* This name was spelled in several ways.

gathered without regard to their *personnel*. The navy was little better. Commodore Saltonstall refused to co-operate with the land forces at the proper time. General Lovell was a brave officer of good reputation, but had not had the necessary experience in actual warfare. General Wadsworth, the second in command was the best officer of the expedition, and his conduct during the whole affair received the approbation of the Committee of Investigation. The general officers were:

Commander in Chief, Brigadier General Solomon Lovell, of Weymouth, Mass.; Second in authority, Brigadier General Peleg Wadsworth, of Duxbury, Mass., afterwards of Portland, Maine. He was the grandfather of the poet H. W. Longfellow. Commander of the Fleet, Commodore Dudley Saltonstall, of New Haven, Conn.

When the attack was made the fort was not half built and the British commander, McLean, expected to surrender to save the lives of his soldiers and it is said he stood by the halyards ready to lower his flag at the proper moment, but because of the conduct of Saltonstall it was not necessary. The expedition was called by the people of Maine, "The Bagaduce Expedition," and ever afterwards was a subject of discussion among them. Maine furnished most of the soldiers and something of the navy. Another expedition was proposed in 1780, but was abandoned by the advice of Washington. The British withdrew from Fort George before January, 1784, and it was the last fort from which the King's forces were embarked, at the end of the war. Most of the Loyalists went to St. Andrews, N. B., where land had been granted them and where sixty or seventy houses were erected for their occupancy. They took down several houses at Castine and re-erected them at St. Andrews.

NATHAN GOOLD.

PORTLAND, ME.

PERSONAL NOTES
DR. JOHN CALEF

This journal was identified as the work of Dr. John Calef by his name appearing on the map. He had taken part in the siege of Louisburg and it is said he left a manuscript account of that event which has been lost. He was an important man in his time.

Dr. Calef, which name was also spelled Calfe, Calf, Caleff and Kaloph, was born in Ipswich, Mass, Aug. 30, 1726, the son of Robert and Margaret (Staniford) Calef. His grandparents were Dr. Joseph and Mary (Ayer) Calef of Ipswich, who were married in Boston, May 2, 1693. The parents of Dr. Joseph were Robert and Mary Calef of Roxbury, Mass. Robert Calef was the author of "More Wonders of the Invisible World," which antagonized Cotton and Increase Mather, about 1692. It was publicly burned on the campus of Harvard College by the orders of the latter, who was then president of the college.

In 1755, the Governor ordered Dr. Calef to Fort Halifax,* on the Kennebec River, now in the town of Winslow, Maine, to attend the sick. He found his services much needed by the garrison and remained about two months. He also went there again in 1772. He engaged, as surgeon, in Colonel Ichabod Plaisted's regiment Feb. 18, 1756, to go to Crown Point, and was discharged Jan. 19, 1757, remaining at the Albany hospital. He served in the Massachusetts General Court before the Revolutionary War, but remained loyal to the King and became obnoxious to the Colonists. He was declared by them a traitor, and a price was set upon his head. By the energy of his wife, he escaped capture and went to St. Andrews, N. B.

* Fort Halifax was at the junction of the Kennebec and Sebasticook rivers in the present town of Winslow, Maine. It was built by Governor William Shirley of Massachusetts in 1755, and was named for the Duke of Halifax. A full history of the Fort by Hon. William Goold, was published in the *Collections* of the Maine Historical Society, First Series, Vol. 8, page 199.

Dr. Calef was active in the Penobscot expedition and was Commissary of the inhabitants in the County of Lincoln, Maine. He was the surgeon at Fort George and acted as chaplain. In 1780, he went to England as an agent of the Penobscot Loyalists. The scheme was that the country between the Saco and the St. Croix Rivers was to be erected into a new province to be called " New Ireland." Thomas Oliver was to be governor, Daniel Leonard, chief justice, and Dr. Calef the clerk of the council at a salary of £50. The land was to be granted to the Loyalists in large tracts to the most meritorious with small grants to the poorest. It was to be a landed country. The English church was to be the established religion. This scheme was approved of by the King and his Cabinet, but was unsuccessful. Dr. Calef remained in England two years, when he revived the effort, but it received its death blow from a decision of the Attorney General of England that it violated the sacredness of the chartered rights of the Province of Massachusetts Bay, and he was informed that it could not be done as " the pressure is too strong."

In 1784, Dr. Calef was one of the grantees of St. Andrews, N. B., and was the first physician to settle there, where he built a house. After the war he was surgeon of the general hospital at St. John, N. B., and was attached to the garrison, then stationed at Fort Howe. After October, 1800, he returned to St. Andrews where he resided until his death, which occurred Oct. 23, 1812, at the age of 86 years.

Dr. Calef married, first, Margaret Rogers, daughter of Rev. Nathaniel and Mary (Leverett) Rogers of Ipswich, who died March 27, 1751; second, Jan. 18, 1753, Dorothy Jewett, daughter of Rev. Jedidiah and Elizabeth (Dummer) Jewett, both of Rowley, Mass. Children by first wife were:

1. Margaret, born Oct. 15, 1748; married Oct. 14, 1767, Dr. Daniel Scott of Boston.

PERSONAL NOTES 11

2. Mary, bapt. March, 1750; married Capt. John Dutch of Ipswich.

By second marriage:

3. John, born Nov. 2, 1753; drowned Feb. 19, 1782.
4. Jedidiah, born Sept. 22, 1755; died March 10, 1778.
5. Elizabeth, born Oct. 25, 1757; died Sept. 7, 1771.
6. Daughter, still-born May 1, 1759.
7. Robert, born Nov. 16, 1760.
8. Dorothy, born Nov. 16, 1762.
9. Sarah, born June 27, 1764; died in St. Andrews, N. B., March 25, 1854, unm.
10. Susanna, born Feb. 7, 1766.
11. A son still-born Jan., 1768.
12. Mehitable, born Sept. 13, 1768; married Capt. David Mowat Nov. 14, 1786, and died at St. Andrews, N. B., Dec. 25, 1860, aged 92 years.
13. Martha, born May 22, 1770; died Sept. 23, 1771.
14. Samuel, born July 20, 1772; alive at 17.
15. Daughter, still-born, April 12, 1775.
16. Daughter, still-born, Aug. 22, 1776.
17. Jedidiah Jewett, born Jan. 22, 1778.

An extended sketch of the Caleff family by David Russell Jack, was published in *Acadiensis,* Vol. 7, p. 261-273, July, 1907, which enabled the writer to verify these facts he had already obtained from other sources.

Dr. John Calef spelled his name with one f, on the map and in his signature to five letters examined by the writer, although the family seemed to have added another f later.

GENERAL FRANCIS McLEAN

Brigadier General Francis McLean, also called a Major-General, whose name was properly spelled MacLean, was the son of Captain William, who was the grandson of Lachlan, the first of the family of Blaich and second of John Crubach, eighth MacLean of Ardgour. As soon as he was able to carry arms Francis obtained a commission in the same regiment with his father, a regiment of Scottish troops maintained in the Dutch service. He was at the siege of Bergen-op-Zoom in 1747, when the French, after a siege of two months, took the place by storm. "Lieutenants Francis and Allan MacLean (third son of Torloisk) of the Scotch brigade were taken prisoners and carried before General Löwendahl, who thus addressed them: 'Gentlemen, consider yourself on parole. If all had conducted themselves as you and your brave corps have done, I should not now be master of Bergen-op-Zoom.'" He was detained prisoner in France for some time; and on his release was promoted to a captaincy and entered the Forty-second Royal Highlanders. At the capture of Gaudaloupe, Francis was severely wounded, but owing to his gallant conduct was promoted to the rank of major and appointed Governor of the island of Marie Galante. He served in Canada under Wolfe but returned to Great Britain and embarked with the expedition for reducing the island of Belleisle on the coast of France. Here he had his right arm shattered and was taken prisoner. On being exchanged, his bravery was rewarded by promotion to the lieutenant-colonelcy of the 82d. In 1762, he was sent to aid the Portuguese against the combined attack of France and Spain. He was made commander of Almeida, a fortified town on the Spanish frontier, which command he held for several years and was nominated to the government of Estremadura and the City of Lisbon. On his leaving Portugal in 1778, the king presented him with a handsomely mounted sword, and the queen gave him a valuable diamond ring. On his return to England he was dispatched to America and appointed to the government of Halifax. He repaired with the army in June, 1779, to Penobscot Bay and proceeded to erect defences. His regiment had arrived at Halifax from England in 1778. After the completion of Fort George, McLean and his regiment returned to Halifax where he died, unmarried, May 4, 1781, in his 64th year and was buried two days later. General McLean was a good officer and left a good impression on those with whom he came in contact on the Penobscot.

GENERAL SOLOMON LOVELL

General Solomon Lovell was born in Abington, Mass., June 1, 1732, and married (1) Jan. 19, 1758, Lydia, daughter of John and Sarah (Hunt) Holbrook, who was born in Weymouth, Mass., Sept. 3, 1734, and died May 21, 1761. She had two children. He married (2) in May, 1762, Hannah, daughter of James and Hannah (Reed) Pittey, born Dec. 8, 1730, and died July 8, 1795. She had seven children. General Lovell was the son of David and Mary (Torrey) Lovell, and a descendant of Robert Lovell who went to Weymouth in 1635. His father was a graduate of Harvard in 1725.

Solomon Lovell was from youth in some official capacity of his town, and became actively engaged in the cause of the Colonies during the Revolution, and was promoted through the different grades to a brigadier-general. He commanded the military division of which Boston was the center. He served under Gen. John Sullivan in Rhode Island and commanded the land forces in the Penobscot Expedition of 1779, and was commended for his services. He died Sept. 9, 1801, aged 69 years. It has been said of him that " he was honest, brave and competent, faithful in all the relations of life, carrying the respect and esteem of all with whom it was his privilege to associate."

BIBLIOGRAPHY.

History of Castine, Maine, Wheeler.
History of Maine, Williamson.
Weymouth, Massachusetts, Historical Society's *Collection,* Vol. II.
Maine Historical Society's *Collections.*
History of Col. Jonathan Mitchell's Cumberland County Regt. 1779, by Nathan Goold.

A JOURNAL

ON the 17th day of June, 1779, Brigadier-General Francis McLean landed at Majabidwaduce (Penobscot), with about 700 of his Majesty's forces, composed of detachments from the 74th* and 82d** regiments, to take post in the eastern country of New England. The time from this day to the 17th of July was taken up in clearing a spot to erect a fort and building the same, and a battery near the shore, with store-houses, etc.

July 18. Intelligence was received that a fleet and army were preparing at Boston to besiege Penobscot, of which but little notice was taken. Capt. Henry Mowat, of his Majesty's sloop *Albany*, having been many years on the American station and well acquainted with the disposition of the inhabitants, and of the importance of the country of Penobscot to the Americans for fire-wood, lumber, masts, cod and river fish, gave credit to the information, and ordered the three sloops of war into the best situation to defend the harbour, annoy the Enemy and co-operate with the land forces.

July 19. The intelligence of yesterday gains credit; whereupon the General, in order to make the proper dispositions for an

---

* The 74th Foot, "The Argyle Highlanders," was raised by the Duke of Hamilton and served in America four years, under John Campbell. Milltown, New Brunswick, and a tract of good farming land on the Digdequash, were granted to the officers and men of this regiment who had been in the garrison on the Penobscot.

** The 82nd Foot, "The Hamilton Regiment," served in America four years and was under Sir William Erskine in 1779. After the completion of Fort George, at Castine, this regiment returned to Halifax with General McLean. Sir John Moore, made famous by Wolfe's poem on his burial in 1809, was then but eighteen, a lieutenant, as was Sir James Craig, who became the Governor General of Canada.

immediate defence, desists for the present from his purpose of proceeding in a regular way with the fort; and prepares to fortify in a manner more expeditious and better suited to the present emergency; in doing which he shows the utmost vigilance and activity, giving every where the necessary directions, visiting incessantly by night and day the different parts of the works, and thus by his example animating his men to proceed, regardless of fatigue, with vigour and alacrity in their operations. The Inspector of the inhabitants begs leave of the General to call in the people to assist in carrying on the works; which being granted, about a hundred inhabitants came in (with their Captain* at their head) as volunteers; and having worked three days gratis, cleared the land of wood in the front of the fort, to the satisfaction of the General, who returned them his thanks.

July 20. All hands busy at work, preparing to receive the enemy. At noon Capt. Mowat, having made every preparation in his power to secure the harbour, &c., sent 180 men on shore from the ships of war, to work on the fort.

July 21. Intelligence is received that a fleet of near 40 sail of vessel had sailed from Boston eastward. All hands at work day and night.

July 22. Nothing remarkable. All hands at work day and night. This evening a spy brought an account that 40 sail of vessel put into Townsend Harbour yesterday.

July 23. Every person busily employed. The Inspector calls a great number of inhabitants to work, who are employed in felling trees, raising an abatis round the fort, building platforms for the guns, &c. Saw three sail in the offing. Several canoes from the islands below come to advise the General of

*John Perkins.

a large number of vessels being becalmed off St. George's Island,* standing with their heads to the eastward. All doubt of an attack from the Enemy is now vanished.

July 24. At 4 P. M. discovered a large fleet standing up the bay, which from various circumstances we believed to be the armament that, according to intelligence received, had been fitted out at Boston to besiege this place. On this account Capt. Mowat thought proper to detain the *North* and *Nautilus* sloops, which had been ordered for other service. At five, by signal from the *Albany,* the seamen who for some days past had been at work raising the S. E. bastion of the fort, repaired on board their respective ships (which were immediately cleared for action) and, as had been usual, were every evening exercised at their quarters. The *Albany, North* and *Nautilus* had dropped down the harbour and moored in a well-formed and close line of battle across the entrance, immediately within the rocks on Bagwaduce point and the point of Nautilus or Cross Island; giving a berth, out of the line of fire, to three transports stationed and prepared to slip and run foul of the Enemy's ships, should they attempt to enter the harbour. The troops were encamped about half a mile from the works; the well bastion of which was not yet begun, nor the Seamen's** quite finished; but on the appearance of the Enemy the works

---

* The St. George Islands are off the mouth of St. Georges River and are a part of the town of St. George, Maine. They were originally a part of the Plantation of St. George, then Cushing, and in 1903 the town of St. George was incorporated. Penobscot Harbor, referred to by Rosier, in 1605, is at Allen's Island and here was the first attempt by Europeans to cultivate the soil of Maine. Captain George Weymouth erected a cross on Allen's Island in 1605, and the Maine Historical Society erected a granite one in 1905 to commemorate the event. The town of St. George is thirteen miles south of Rockland.

** So called as being the work of the seamen only under the direction of Lieut. William Brooke, of his Majesty's ship *North*.

were put in a more defensible state, some cannon were mounted, and the little army was in garrison early the next morning. Guard-boats, during the night, watched the motions of the Enemy, who were discovered to have come to an anchor about three or four leagues off, in the narrows of Penobscot.

July 25. At 10 A. M. a brig appeared at some distance from the harbour's mouth, and after reconnoitering the situation of the men of war, stood back into the fleet. At noon the Enemy's fleet, consisting of 37 sail of ships, brigs and transports, arrived in the bay of the harbour; the transports proceeded about half a mile up Penobscot river, and came to an anchor, while the armed ships and brigs stood off and on and a boat from each ship repaired on board their flagship, which had thrown thrown out a signal for that purpose.

At 3 P. M., nine ships, forming into three divisions, stood towards the King's ships and, as they advanced in the line, hove-to, and engaged. A very brisk cannonade continued four glasses*, when the Enemy bore up, and came to an anchor in the bay without. The King's ships suffered only in their rigging. The fire of the Enemy was random and irregular, and their manoevres, as to backing and filling, bespoke confusion, particularly in the first division, which scarcely got from the line of fire when the second began to engage. The second and third divisions appeared to have but one object in view, that of cutting the springs of the men of war, to swing them from the bearings of their broadsides, and thereby to afford their fleet an entrance into the harbour. During the cannonade with the shipping the Enemy made an attempt to land their troops on Bagwaduce, but were repulsed with some loss. On the retreat of the Enemy's troops and

*A " glass " is a marine measure of time, equal to half an hour.

ships the garrison manned their works, and gave three cheers to the men-of-war, which were returned; and soon after the general and field-officers went down to the beach and also gave three cheers, which were returned by the ships.

Guard-boats and ships' companies during the night lay at their quarters.

July 26. At 10 A. M. the Enemy's ships got under weigh, and forming their divisions as yesterday, stood in and engaged the King's ships four glasses and a half. The damages sustained this day, also, were chiefly in the rigging at the extreme ends of the ships; and the fire of the Enemy appears again to be directed to the moorings; which attempt not proving successful, they bore up and anchored without. The Enemy again attempted to land their troops, but were driven back with some little loss. At 6 P. M. the Enemy, having stationed two brigs of 14 guns and one sloop of 12, on the east side of Nautilus Island, landed 200 men, and dislodging a party of 20 marines, took possession of four 4-pounders (two not mounted) and a small quantity of ammunition. At 9 P. M. it being found that the Enemy were very busy at work, and that they had landed some heavy artillery which they were getting up to the height of the island, and against which the men-of-war could not act in their present station, it was judged expedient to move them farther up the river. This was accordingly done, and the line formed as before: the transports moved up at the same time and anchored within the men-of-war. Guard-boats and the ships' companies, as usual, lying at their quarters.

July 27. Pretty quiet all this day. A few shot from some ships of the Enemy were aimed at the small battery on Majabigwaduce point, which were returned with a degree of success, one ship having been driven from her station. Observed the

Enemy very busy in erecting their battery on Nautilus Island. The garrison being much in want of cannon, some guns from the transports and from the off-side of the men-of-war, were landed, and being dragged by the seamen up to the fort, were disposed of for its use. At 3 P. M. a boat passing from the Enemy's ships to Nautilus island was sunk by a random shot from the fort. At 11 P. M. the guard-boats from the King's ships fell in and exchanged a few shots with the Enemy's.

July 28. At 3 A. M. under their ships' fire, the Enemy made good their landing on Majabigwaduce, and from their great superiority of numbers obliged the King's troops to retreat to the garrison. The Enemy's right pressed hard and in force upon the left of the King's troops, and attempted to cut off a party of men at the small battery; but the judgment and experience of a brave officer (Lieut. Caffrac, of the 82nd) counteracted their designs, and a retreat was effected with all the order and regularity necessary on such occasions. An attempt was made to demolish the guns, but the Enemy pushed their force to this ground so rapidly as not to suffer it. The possession of this battery afforded their ships a nearer station, on which they immediately seized. At 6 A. M. the Enemy opened their battery of 18 and 12 pounders from Nautilus island, and kept up the whole day a brisk and well-directed fire against the men-of-war. The King's ships cannonaded the battery for two glasses, and killed some men at it; but their light metal (six pounders) was found to be of little service, in comparison to the damages they sustained from such heavy metal brought against them. At 10 A. M., the *Warren,* of 32 guns, the Commodore's ship, and which had not as yet been in action, got under weigh and with three more ships shewed an appearance of entering the harbour, but hauled by the wind at a long distance. A brisk fire was kept up for half an hour, when the Enemy bore up and came to an anchor again without. The *Warren* suffered considerably: her mainmast shot through in two places, the gammoning of her bowsprit cut to pieces, and her forestay shot away. Their confusion appeared to be great, and very nearly occasioned her getting on shore, so that they were obliged to let go an anchor and drop into the inlet between Majabigwaduce head and the point; where the ship lay this and the next day repairing her damages. The battery on the island still keeping up a heavy fire, and the ships' crews being exposed without the least benefit to the service, Capt. Mowat thought proper to move further up the harbour; which was done in the night and the line formed again; he being firmly resolved to dispute the harbour to the last extremity, as on that entirely depended the safety of the garrison, whose communication with the men-of-war was of the utmost importance. The dispositions on shore and on the water co-operating, and perfectly supporting each other, foiled the Enemy in their purposes; their troops were yet confined to a spot they could not move from, and while the harbour was secure their intentions of making approaches and investing the fort on all sides could by no means be put in execution. The present station of the men-of-war being such as rendered it impossible for the Enemy's ships to act but at particular periods, the marines (whose service in their peculiar line of duty was not immediately required on board) were ordered on shore to garrison duty, holding themselves in readiness to embark at a moment's notice, which with ease they could have effected in ten or fifteen minutes. Guard-boats as usual during the night.

July 29. At 6 A. M. the Enemy's ships weighed, and altering their positions, came to an anchor again. The State of the fortress requiring more cannon, some remaining off-side guns were landed from the men-of-war and dragged by the seamen up to the fortress for its use and that of the batteries; and though the task to be performed, up a steep hill, over rocks and innumerable stumps of fallen trees, was laborious, yet their chearfulness and zeal for the service surmounted every difficulty. P. M. the Enemy opened their batteries on the heights of Majabigwaduce, and kept up a warm and incessant fire against the fortress. The commanding ground of the Enemy's works and the short distance from the fortress, gave them some advantages with their grape as well as round shot which considerably damaged the storehouse in the garrison. Six pieces of cannon at the half-moon battery near Banks' house, and which belonged to the fortress, being now found necessary for its particular defence, were moved up to it and replaced with some ship's guns, under the direction of the gunner of the *Albany,* with a party of seamen Capt. Mowat having obtained intelligence that the Enemy, in despair of reducing the King's ships by the means of their own, or of getting possession of the harbour, had come to the resolution of joining their whole force in troops, marines and seamen, to storm the fortress the next morning at day-break, he judged it expedient to re-inforce the garrison with what seamen could be conveniently spared; and for this purpose, at the close of the evening, 140 men under the command of Lieut. Brooke, were sent into garrison: part of them were immediately detached to re-inforce the troops on the out-line piquets, others manned the facing of their own bastion, while the remainder were busily employed in raising the cavaliers in the fort. In all these operations a brotherly affection appeared to unite the forces both by sea and land, and to direct their views all to one point, much to their credit and to the honour and benefit of the service. During the night the Enemy threw a number of shells into the fortress. At 10

P. M. a few shot between the Enemy's guard-boats and those from the King's ships.

July 30. The Enemy's ships preserve their disposition of yesterday. A brisk cannonade the whole day between the fortress and the Enemy's batteries on the height, and a number of shells thrown on both sides. The storehouse being apprehended to be in danger, some seamen were ordered to move the provisions out of the fortress into the ditch in its rear; as likewise a quantity at another storehouse. Guard-boats as usual.

July 31. At 2 A. M. the seamen and marines of the Enemy's fleet landed to the westward of the half-moon battery, and under cover of the night attacked the piquet, and by heavy platoon firings obliged them to retreat; but an alert re-inforcement of 50 men who were detached from the garrison, under the command of Lieut. Graham* of the 82nd regiment, to the support of the piquet, drove the Enemy back with some loss in killed, wounded and taken, amounting on the whole, according to the best information, to about 100; the loss on the part of the King's forces, amounting to 13 killed, wounded and missing, fell chiefly on the seamen and marines, who composed the piquet this night. Lieut. Graham unfortunately received a dangerous wound in this action.

August 1. A slack fire on all sides. At 4 P. M. the Enemy's fleet getting under weigh, and the wind and tide serving them to enter the harbour, the embodied seamen were immediately called on board their respective ships; but it afterward appeared that the Enemy weighed only to form a closer line. Guard-boats as usual.

August 2. At 10 A. M. three of the Enemy's ships weighed and

*John Graham, 82d Regiment.

came to an anchor nearer the harbour's mouth. Some cannonading between the fortress and the Enemy's batteries on the height. The outer magazine of the fortress being too much exposed, as lying in front and between the two fires, the marines were charged with the duty of bringing it to the magazine in the fortress; which was performed without any loss. P. M. a flag of truce from the Enemy, to treat for the exchange of a lieutenant of their fleet taken (wounded) at the half-moon battery on the 31st ult., but he had died of his wounds this morning. This day the Enemy posted some marksmen behind trees within musquet-shot of the fortress, and killed and wounded some centinels.

August 3. A slack fire the whole day. Perceived the Enemy busy in erecting a battery to the northward on the main above the King's ships. By a deserter from the Enemy's fleet we learn the force landed below the half-moon battery was 1000 seamen and marines, joined on their landing by 200 troops; that their intentions were to storm the fortress in the rear while the army from the heights made their attack in front; that it was not intended to storm the half-moon battery, but that they had mistaken their road in endeavoring to get in the rear of the fortress, when they received the first fire of the piquet, which led them to suppose their design had been discovered, and that they were ambushed. The army also, believing this to be the case, retreated to their ground. At 2 P. M. some seamen were sent to the fortress to assist in working the cannon, and another party for the defence of the Seamen's bastion, where a number of swivels from the men-of-war were planted, loaded with grape-shot, as a precaution against any attempt of the Enemy to storm the works. By request of the General a number of pikes were also brought from the King's ships to the fortress, and put in the hands of the seamen, to prevent the Enemy from BOARDING their bastion. Guard-boats as usual.

August 4. The Enemy's ships retain their former situation. A smart cannonading between the fortress and the batteries on the heights, and a great number of shells thrown on both sides. Some ships' buckets for the use of the garrison brought on shore, in case the fascines at the well bastion, or store houses might be fired by the Enemy's shells. At 9 A. M. the Enemy opened their new battery near Wescoat's house, on the main, to the northward of the shipping. A brisk fire was kept up the whole day, and the men-of-war suffered much in their hulls and rigging; being too far from the battery for the light metal of the ships to produce any effect, their companies were ordered below. P. M. some skirmishing between the piquets, and trifling losses on both sides, on the Enemy's some Indians were killed.

During the day several accidents happened by cannon shot in the fort; among others the boatswain of the *Nautilus* was wounded by grape, and a seaman belonging to the *North* killed by an 18-pounder, at the guns they were stationed at in the fortress.

August 5. Cannonading the greatest part of the day between the fortress and the Enemy's batteries on the height, and from the north battery against the men-of-war, damaging their hulls and rigging. A. M. the remaining off-side guns from his Majesty's sloop *North* brought on shore, and mounted in the cavalier in the fortress. P. M. the garrison, being much in want of wads and match, was supplied from the men-of-war, as also with some six-pound shot, in which it is deficient. The north battery on the main having the command of the opposite shore on the peninsula of Majabigwaduce, where the Enemy, under its protection, might make lodgements in their approaches toward the heights opposite the men-of-war and within shot of the fortress, and might thereby destroy the communication between them and the garrison, Capt. Mowat judged it necessary to erect a work in order to preserve this communication: a square redoubt was therefore marked out, to be manned with 50 seamen and to mount eight ships' guns *en barbette.* Guard-boats as usual during the night.

August 6. Slack fire between the fortress and batteries on the heights, and a few shot from the north battery against the men-of-war, cutting their rigging and dismounting a six-pounder on board the *North.* At 4 A. M. 70 seamen from the different ships, under the direction of Lieut. Brooke, of the *North,* sent on shore to raise the Seamen's redoubt on the height. P. M. a quantity of musquet-cartridges (of which the garrison was in want) brought on shore from the men-of-war. Guard-boats as usual. At 11 a few shot exchanged between the guard-boats.

August 7. The Enemy's ships preserve their positions. At 9 A. M. three of their brigs got under weigh and stood down the bay, supposed on the look-out. Some skirmishing between the piquets, with loss to the Enemy; Lieut. McNeil,* of the 82d, and one private, wounded. Slack fire between the batteries and the fortress, and the north battery perfectly silent. At 4 P. M. discovered a boat crossing the S. E. bay to Hainey's plantation, where the Enemy kept a piquet. Lieut. Congalton,† of the *Nautilus* chaced with the boats from the men-of-war, and took her; but her crew, with those of a whale-boat and a gondola for transportating cannon, got safe on shore and joined the piquet. Capt. Farnham ‡ of the *Nau-*

*Roderick McNeil.
†Andrew Congalton.
‡Thomas Farnham, Navy List, 1779.

tilus, with Lieut. Brooke and 50 seamen, joined by a party of soldiers from the garrison, landed and scoured the woods; the Enemy fled immediately, and so effectually concealed themselves as not to be discovered; some had left their arms ammunition and blankets, which were taken and brought on board.

Guard-boats as usual during the night.

By a deserter from the Enemy we learn that General Lovell had sent out small parties from his army, round the country, and brought in a great number of loyal inhabitants, who were sent on board their fleet and thrust down the holds heavily laden with irons, both on the hands and feet; their milch cows and other stock killed for the Enemy's use; all their moveables destroyed or plundered, and their wives and children left destitute of every support of life.

August 8. A constant cannonade the whole day between the fortress and the Enemy's batteries on the height, and from the north battery against the men-of-war, but returned only with a musquet. At 10 A. M. the Enemy brought a field-piece to play from the main on the seamen working at the redoubt; but the facing towards the Enemy being the first raised, for the purpose of covering the party, it was impossible to dislodge them; and a covering party daily attending from the garrison prevented a nearer approach on any other ground. This evening the redoubt was finished, and to the credit of the seamen, met with the approbation of the General and Engineers. Guard-boats as usual.

August 9. Cannonading as usual. At 9 A. M. a new battery, on the left of the Enemy's lines, was opened against the fortrees, and its chief fire, as well as the shells, directed against the N. W. bastion, raised with fascines only. P. M. discovered the Enemy had moved their piquet from Hainey's plantation, and given up their design of carrying on a work for two 18-pounders against the men-of-war.

Guard-boats as usual during the night.

August 10. The Enemy's ships in the former position. A slack fire on all sides, and nothing material.

August. 11. A smart cannonading from all the batteries, and some shot from the north battery well directed at the men-of war.

August 12. Slack fire on all sides, and no material operations the whole day; but at 9 P. M. a large body of seamen and marines from the Enemy's fleet landed below Banks' * house to the westward, and setting fire to some barns, houses, and a quantity of lumber-boards, &c., on the beach, retreated to their ships again.

August 13. At day break some skirmishing between the piquets, but no material loss on either side. At 1 P. M. came in some deserters from the Enemy's ships, who say the boat chaced on shore at Hainey's plantation had in her their Commodore and some officers of their fleet, who, having escaped, returned to their ships after lying two days and a night in the woods; that one of the officers (Capt. Ross, of the *Monmouth*) had broke his leg in the woods; and that they were much disconcerted at the loss of the gondola, which was intended to carry over some 18-pounders to the battery on the plantation.

Capt. Mowat also (by his usual diligence) obtained information that a degree of mutiny prevailed in the Enemy's fleet against their Commodore who, notwithstanding the re-

*The home of Aaron Banks, a soldier of the French and Indian wars, who came from York, Maine, in 1765. He married Mary Perkins of York, who was a sister of John and Daniel Perkins of Bagaduce. He died August 9, 1823, at Penobscot, where he moved after peace was declared. He has no descendants of his name. Banks and his family were detained for upwards of three weeks as prisoners on board the British sloop *North*.

solves of several councils of war and urgent solicitations of the General to make another attempt on the King's ships, had hitherto declined it through fear of losing some ships; but that, in consequence of another council held this morning on the *Warren,* it was determined to force the harbour next tide and take or destroy the men-of-war; that five ships were destined for this service, one of which was the *Warren;* but that the *Putnam,* of 20 guns, was to lead, and that each ship was doubly manned with picked men. This information was confirmed at noon by five of their fleet getting under weigh and coming to an anchor in a line, the *Putnam* being the headmost ship. The marines were now called on board their respective ships, the barricades strengthened, guns double-shotted and every disposition made for the most vigorous defence. The *St. Helena* transport had been brought into the line and fitted out with what guns could be procured, and the crews of the transports (now scuttled and laid on shore to prevent them from falling into the Enemy's hands), turned on board to fight her; and the General had also advanced five pieces of cannon, under cover of an *épaulement,* to salute them as they came in. But at 5 P. M. the appearance of some strange sails in the offing disconcerted the Enemy's plan, and the five ships, getting under weigh again, stood off and on the whole night. Guard-boats watching the motions of the Enemy's fleet, and the ships' companies standing at their quarters until daylight. This night had been fixed upon to storm the north battery with 60 seamen under the command of Lieut. Brooke, supported by Lieut. Caffrac of the 82d, with 50 soldiers; but the Enemy's operations, and the appearance of the strange fleet, prevented the execution of it.

August 14. At day-break this morning it was discovered that the Enemy had during the night moved off their cannon, and quitting the heights of Majabigwaduce, silently embarked in small vessels. At 4 A. M. after firing a shot or two, they also evacuated Nautilus island; and leaving their cannon spiked and dismounted, got on board a brig lying to receive them, and made sail with the transports up Penobscot river. The whole fleet now got under weigh, and upon one of the brigs heaving in sight off the harbour's mouth, with various signals aboard, they bore up with all sail after the transports. There now remaining no doubt but the strange fleet was the relief expected, the off-side guns of the *Albany, North* and *Nautilus* were got down from the fortress, and being taken on board, the three ships slipped their stern moorings, hove up their bower anchors, and working out of the harbour joined in about the centre of the King's fleet, in pursuit of the flying enemy, who were now crowding with every sail they could set. The *Hunter* and *Hampden,* two of the Enemy's ships, of 20 guns each, attempted to escape through the passage of Long Island,* but were cut off and taken; the former ran in shore all standing, and was instantly deserted by her crew, who got safe on shore; and the *Raisonable,* Sir George Collier, being the sternmost ship in the fleet, took possession and got her off, and came to an anchor near her. The rest of his Majesty's ships continued in chace of the Enemy until it grew so dark as to render the narrow navigation exceedingly dangerous; and they were obliged to anchor for the night, while the Enemy, having good pilots, ran some miles further up the river. The *Defiance* brig, of 14 guns, ran into an inlet where she could not be pursued, and was set on fire by her crew. During the night the Enemy set fire to several ships and brigs, which blew up with vast explosions.

In short, the harmony and good understanding that sub-

* Long Island, now the town of Islesborough, is about twelve miles long, contains about six thousand acres and is in Penobscot Bay, four miles from Castine.

sisted amongst the Forces by sea and by land—enabled them to effect almost prodigies; for so ardently did they vie with each other in the general service that it may be truly said not a single Officer, Sailor or Soldier was once seen to shrink from his duty, difficult and hazardous as it was. The flying scout, of 50 men commanded by Lieut. Caffrac of the 82d, in particular distinguished themselves to admiration, marching frequently almost round the peninsula, both by day and by night, and with drum and fife playing the tune called *Yankee,* which greatly dispirited the Enemy, and prevented their small parties from galling our men at the works. In one instance they even drove back to their incampment 300 of the Enemy who had been sent to storm an outwork.

The manoeuvres of the three Sloops of War, under the direction of Capt. Mowat, were moreover such as enabled the King's forces to hold out a close siege of 21 days, against a fleet and army of more than six times their number and strength; insomuch that on the first appearance of the re-inforcement from New York in the offing, the Enemy debarked their troops and sailed with their whole fleet up Penobscot river, where they burnt their shipping and from thence marched to their respective homes; and the loyal inhabitants, who were taken in the time of the siege and cruelly treated on board their ships, had their irons taken off and were set at liberty.*

Thus did this little Garrison,† with three Sloops of War,

*To give them a cool airing, as the enemy called it, once a day the irons were knocked off their feet and they were put into a boat alongside the ship, where they remained about an hour, and had the filth of the ship poured upon their heads.

†When the account of an army coming to besiege this place was received, the curtains in some parts of the intended fort were not more than four feet in height; two bastions were but just begun to be built, and the other two were only marked out.

by the unwearied exertions of Soldiers and Seamen whose bravery cannot be too much extolled, under the judicious conduct of Officers whose zeal is hardly to be paralleled, succeed in an enterprise of great importance, against difficulties apparently insurmountable, under circumstances exceedingly critical, and in a manner strongly expressive of their faithful and spirited attachment to the interests of their King and Country.

A LIST of the Enemy's Ships, etc., taken and destroyed in Penobscot River

Ships' Names	Commanders	Guns	No. of Men	Metal Pounders	
Warren	Saltonstall	32	250	18 and 12	Burnt
Sally	Holmes	22	200	9 and 6	Burnt
Putnam	Waters	20	130	9	Burnt
Hector	Cairns	20	130	9	Burnt
Revenge	Hallet	20	120	6	Burnt
Monmouth	Ross	20	100	6	Burnt
Hampden	Salter	20	130	9 and 6	Taken
Hunter	Brown	20	130	6	Taken
Vengeance	Thomas	18	140	9 and 6	Burnt
Black Prince	West	18	100	6	Burnt
Sky Rocket	Burke	16	120	6	Burnt

BRIGS

Ships' Name	Commanders	No. of Guns	No. of Men	Metal Pounders	
Hazard	Williams	18	100	6	Burnt
Active		16	100	6	Burnt
Tyrannicide	Cathcart	14	90	6	Burnt
Defiance		14	90	6	Burnt
Diligence	Brown	14	90	4	Burnt
Pallas	Johnstone	14	80	4	Burnt
Sloop Providence	Hacker	12	50	6	Burnt

With Nine Sail of Transport Vessels ....Taken
And Ten Sail of Transport and Ordnance ditto ....Burnt
Total   37

320

Killed, wounded and missing, of His Majesty's Sea and
  Land Forces 70
Killed, wounded and taken, on the Enemy's Side 474

Of the captains of these vessels the Massachusetts records show particulars. The *Sally* is described as the *Charming Sally*, a privateer owned by William Erskine of Boston. Captain Alexander Holmes was afterwards captain of the privateer *Batchelor*.

William Burke commanded the *Skyrocket*, which was a privateer owned by Ebenezer Parsons, of Boston.

James Johnston was the captain of the *Pallas*, privateer, owned by William Erskine and others, of Boston.

Nathan Brown, of Salem, commanded the *Hunter*, a privateer owned by Bartholomew Putnam. Later he had the privateer-ship *Jack*.

John Cathcart, captain of the *Tyrannicide*, afterward had command of the State ship *Tartar* and another of the same name, a Boston privateer.

John Carnes (not Cairns) had the ship *Hector*, a Boston privateer owned by Jonathan Peale, and afterward of the *Montgomery* and *Porus*, both privateers.

Allen (or John Allen) Hallet, of the *Active*, a State vessel, was afterward in command of the *Tartar* and the *Franklin* and *Minerva*, privateers.

Captain Hoysteed Hacker commanded the *Providence* and afterward the privateer ship *Bucanier*.

Nathanel West was captain of the *Black Prince*, privateer owned by George Williams, of Salem. He afterwards had the *Three Sisters*, owned by Nathaniel Silsbee and Elias Hasket Derby of Salem, and of the *Marquis*.

Daniel Waters was captain of the *General Putnam*, which was owned by Nathaniel Shaw. He had previously commanded the *Lee* and afterwards had the *Friendship*.

PROCLAMATION

By Brigadier-General FRANCIS MCLEAN and ANDREW BARKLEY, Esq., Commanding detachments of his Majesty's Land and Naval Forces in the River Penobscot.

WHEREAS it is well known that there are in the several Colonies in North America, now in open rebellion, many persons who still retain a sense of their duty, and who are only deterred

321

from an open profession of it by the fear of becoming objects of the cruel treatment which they have seen exercised on others, by persons who having plunged their country into the horrors and distresses it now labours under, industriously seize every opportunity of gratifying their avaritious and wicked dispositions by the wanton oppression of individuals:

And whereas it hath been represented that the greater part of the inhabitants on the river Penobscot, and the several islands therein, are well affected to his Majesty's person and the ancient constitution under which they formerly flourished, and from the restoration of which they can alone expect relief from the distressed situation they are now in:

Their Excellencies the Commanders in Chief of his Majesty's naval and land forces in North-America, taking the good dispositions of the inhabitants above mentioned (as represented to them) into their consideration, and desirous of encouraging and protecting the persons professing them, and securing them from any molestation on that account, have ordered here the forces under our respective commands for that purpose: We therefore, in obedience to their directions, hereby invite and urgently request the inhabitants on the river Penobscot and the islands therein in general, to be the first to return to that state of good order and government to which the whole must in the end submit, and openly to profess that loyalty and allegiance from which they have been led to swerve by arguments and apprehensions, of the falsehood of which they must have been long ago sensible, as well as of the views of those who first promoted them. We also call on all those whose principles have never been shaken, to embrace the present opportunity of manifesting them without dread or apprehensions, as we hereby assure them of every protection in the power of the forces under our respective commands to bestow. And, to quiet the apprehensions of any persons who might be deterred from embracing this opportunity by the dread of being punished for any former acts of rebellion which they may have been led to commit, we hereby declare that we will extend our protection, and give every encouragement, to all persons of whatever denomination who shall, within eight days from the date hereof, take the oaths of allegiance and fidelity to his Majesty, before such persons as we shall appoint, either at the headquarters of his Majesty's troops at Majabigwaduce Neck, or at Fort Pownal*; which oaths of allegiance and fidelity we require all persons whatever to come and take within the required time, and not, by neglecting to give such testimony of their loyalty, give room to look upon them as desirous of continuing in an obstinate and unavailing rebellion, and subject themselves to the treatment such conduct will deserve.

To all persons who by returning to their allegiance shall merit it, we not only promise protection and encouragement, with the relief that shall be in our power to alleviate their present distresses, but we also declare that we will employ the forces under our command to punish all persons whatever who shall attempt in any manner to molest them, either in person or property, on account of their loyalty or conduct toward us; and if forced by their behaviour to punish any men or set of men, on the above-mentioned account, we declare that we will do it in such an exemplary manner as we hope will deter others from obliging us to have recourse to such severe means in future.

And whereas the inhabitants to whom this proclamation is addressed, as well as those in general settled in that part of the country called the Province of Maine, have settled themselves on lands, and cultivated them, without any grant or title by which their possession can be secured to them or their posterity; we therefore declare that we have full power to promise, and

* See p. 45.

we do hereby promise, that no person whatever who shall take the oaths of allegiance as above required, and give such other testimony of their attachment to the constitution as we, or other officers commanding his Majesty's forces may require, shall be disturbed in their possessions; but that whenever civil government takes place, they shall receive gratuitous grants from his Majesty (who alone has the power of giving them) of all lands they may have actually cultivated and improved.

And whereas the leaders of the present rebellion, in pursuit of the views which first instigated them to foment it, and probably to blind the people with regard to the cause of the severe distress under which they now labour, have industriously propagated a notion that the officers of his Majesty's sea and land forces willingly add to their sufferings: We, therefore, to remove such prejudices and as far as in us lies to alleviate the misery of the inhabitants of the villages and islands along the coast of New England, hereby declare that such of them as behave themselves in a peaceable, orderly manner, shall have full liberty to fish in their ordinary coast fishing craft without any molestation on our part; on the contrary, they shall be protected in it by all vessels and parties under our command.

Given on board his Majesty's ship *Blonde,* in Majabigwaduce river, the 15th of June, 1779.

FRANCIS MCLEAN,
ANDREW BARKLEY.

PROCLAMATION

By SOLOMON LOVELL, Esq., Brigadier-General and Commander in Chief of the Forces of the State of Massachusetts Bay, and employed on an Expedition against the Army of the King of Great Britain at Penobscot.

WHEREAS it hath been represented to Government that an armament of some sea and land forces belonging to the King of

Great Britain, under the encouragement of divers of inhabitants of these parts, inimicably disposed to the United States of America, have made a descent on Penobscot, and the parts adjacent; and after propagating various false reports of a general insurrection of the Eastern and Northern Indians in their favour, a Proclamation has been issued on the 15th of June last, signed Francis McLean and Andrew Barclay, said to be in behalf and by authority of said King, promising grants of lands which he never owned, and of which he has now forfeited the jurisdiction by an avowed breach of that compact between him and his subjects, whereon said jurisdiction was founded, and terrifying by threatenings which his power in this land is unable to execute, unless his servants have recourse to their wonted methods of midnight slaughter and savage devastation, all designs to induce the free inhabitants of these parts of the State to submit to their power, and to take an oath of allegiance to their King, whereby they must greatly profane the name of God and solemnly entangle themselves in an obligation to give up their cattle, provisions and labour to the will of every officer pretending the authority of said King, and finally to take arms against their brethren whenever called upon; and it appears some persons have been induced out of fear and by the force of compulsion, to take said oath, who may so far be imposed on as to think themselves bound to act in conformity thereto:

I have thought proper to issue this Proclamation, hereby declaring that the allegiance due to the *ancient constitution* obliges to resist to the last extremity the present system of tyranny in the British Government, which has now overset it; that by this mode of government the people have been reduced to a state of nature, and it is utterly unlawful to require any obedience to their forfeited authority; and all acts recognizing such authority are sinful in their nature; no oaths promising it can be lawful; since if any act be sin in itself, no oath can make it a duty; the very taking of such an oath is a crime, of which every act adhering to it is a repetition with dreadful aggravations.

In all cases where oaths are imposed, and persons compelled to submit to them by threats of immediate destruction which they cannot otherwise avoid, it is manifest that, however obligatory they may be to the conscience of the *compeller,* whose interest and meaning is thereby so solemnly witnessed, it *can have no force on the compelled,* whose interest was known, by the compulsion itself, to be the very reverse of the words in which it is expressed.

At the same time, I do assure the inhabitants of Penobscot and the country adjacent, that if they are found to be so lost to all the virtues of good citizens as to comply with advice of said pretended Proclamation (p. 33) by becoming the first to desert the cause of freedom of virtue and of God, which the whole force of Britain and all its auxiliaries now find themselves unable to overthrow, they must expect also to be the first to experience the just resentment of this injured and betrayed Country, in the condign punishment which their treason deserves. From this punishment their invaders will be very unlike to protect them, as it is now known they are not able to protect themselves in any part of America. And as the protection on which those proclaiming Gentlemen say they have *power* only to *promise,* can be afforded by nothing but the forces which they command, and of these forces by the blessing of God, I doubt not in a very short time to be put in possession; so there is more reason to expect it from the Indian members of the community and treated accordingly, anything nations around, as good part of them are now in my encampment, and several hundreds more on their way speedily to join me; and I have the best evidences from all the rest, that they steadfastly refused to accept of any presents, sign the papers, or do any the barbarous acts assigned them by our Enemies; and on the contrary hold themselves in readiness, on the shortest notice, to turn out for the defence of any place which these men may attack.

Therefore, as the authority committed to me necessitates my executing my best endeavours to rid this much-abused country, not only of its foreign but also from its domestic enemies, I do, therefore, declare that when, by the blessing of Heaven on the American arms, we shall have brought the forces that have invaded us to the state they deserve, it shall be my care that the laws of this state be duly executed upon such inhabitants thereof as have traitoriously abetted or encouraged them in their lawless attempts.

And, that proper discrimination may be made between them and the faithful and liege subjects of the United States, I further declare that all persons within the Eastern country, that have taken the oath prescribed by the Enemy, and shall not within forty-eight hours after receiving notice of this proclamation repair to my camp at Majabigwaduce, with such arms and accoutrements as they now possess, shall be considered as traitors who have voluntarily combined with the Common Enemy in the common ruin; but all such as shall appear at head-quarters within said term, and give proper testimony of their determination to continue cordially in allegiance to the United States of America, shall be recognized as good and faithful members of the community and treated accordingly, anything obnoxious in their taking the oath notwithstanding.

Given at the Head-Quarters on the Heights
of Majabigwaduce, this 29th day of July, Anno

Domini, 1779, and in the Fourth Year of the Independence of America.

(Signed) S. LOVELL,
Brig. Gen.

By Command of the General,
JOHN MARSTON, Secretary.

Copy of General LOVELL's Letter to Commodore SALTONSTALL; taken with other Papers on board the Transport.

Head Quarters, Majabigwaduce Heights, Aug. 11, 1779.

SIR,

IN this alarming posture of affairs, I am once more obliged to request the most speedy service in your department; and that a moment be no longer delayed to put in execution what I have been given to understand was the determination of your last council. The destruction of the Enemy's ships must be effected at any rate, although it might cost us half our own; but I cannot possibly conceive that danger, or that the attempt will miscarry. I mean not to determine on your mode of attack; but it appears to me so very practicable that any further delay must be infamous; and I have it this moment by a deserter from one of their ships, that the moment you enter the harbour they will destroy them; which will effectually answer our purpose.

The idea of more batteries against them was sufficiently reprobated; and, would the situation of ground admit of such proceeding, it would *now* take up *dangerous time;* and we have already experienced their obstinacy in that respect.

You cannot but be sensible of my ardent desire to co-operate with you; and of this the guard at Westcot's is a sufficient proof, and which I think a hazardous distance from my encampment. My situation is confined; and while the Enemy's ships are safe, the operations of the Army cannot possibly be extended an inch beyond the present limits; the alternative now remains, to destroy the ships, or raise the siege.

The information of the British ships at the Hook* (probably sailed before this) is not to be despised; not a moment is to be lost; we must determine instantly, or it may be productive of disgrace, loss of ships and men; as to the troops, their retreat is secure, though I would die to save the necessity of it.

I feel for the honour of America, in an expedition which a nobler exertion had long before this crowned with success; and I have now only to repeat the absolute necessity of undertaking the destruction of the ships, or quitting the place; and with these opinions I shall impatiently wait your answer.

I am,
Sir,
Yours, etc.,
S. LOVELL, Brig. Gen.

To Commodore Saltonstall.

POSTSCRIPT

INASMUCH as the Country of Penobscot has till lately been but little known or considered by Britons, the Editor has thought proper to give the public the following short Account of it; having of late years travelled eight times through the same, and made himself acquainted with the most respectable persons in each town, and with the minutest circumstances which respect that District.

Penobscot, sometimes called the Territory of Sagadahock, lies in the eastern part of the Province of Massachusetts Bay, having

* Sandy Hook, New York Harbor. [ED.]
—The "Postscript" was written by Dr. Calef.

the Province of Nova Scotia (viz. Passamaquodie) for its Eastern, the Province of Main (viz. Kennebeck River) its Western, Canada its Northern, and the Ocean its Southern boundary; and is nearly as large as the Kingdom of Ireland. The French were formerly in possession of part of this Country, viz. from Penobscot River eastward: they had a Fort on the Peninsula of Majabigwaduce, commanded by Monsieur Castine, and a great number of French inhabitants settled up Penobscot, and on other rivers, and along the seacoast to Nova Scotia. On the reduction of Louisburg, in the year 1745 Monsieur Castine demolished the Fort; and all the inhabitants of this district broke up, and removed to Canada.

At the end of the last war, viz. in 1763, the General Assembly of Massachusetts Bay granted thirteen Townships, each of six miles square, lying on the east side of Penobscot River, to thirteen companies of Proprietors, who proceeded to lay out the said Townships, and returned plans thereof to the General Assembly, which were approved and accepted. In consequence of this measure about sixty families settled on each Township, and made great improvements of the land. Those settlers employed the then agent for the said province at the Court of Great Britain, to solicit the Royal approbation of those grants; and in the year 1773, as also in the last year (1780) they sent an agent expressly on their own account, for the same purpose, and further to pray that His Majesty would be graciously pleased to sever that District from the Province of Massachusetts Bay, and erect it into a Government under the authority of the Crown; which solicitation has hitherto, however, been without effect.

The inhabitants of this country are in general loyal, except those of the Township of Machias,* who have at that place a small fort under the direction of Congress, and about 135 Indian war-

* This township was granted by the General Assembly ten years after the first thirteen Townships were granted.

riors of the Machias tribe, in their interest; all the other tribes of Northern Indians are in the King's peace.

The soil of this Country is good and well adapted to the culture of every sort of English grain, as well as hemp, flax, etc., but is more especially proper for grassing (in which it excels every other part of America) and for breeding cattle, sheep, swine and horses. Its woods abound with moose † and other kinds of deer, beaver and several kinds of game good for food.

A few miles from the sea-coast are large tracts of land, covered with pine trees, suitable for masts of the largest size.‡ Timber for ship-building, staves, boards, and all other sorts of lumber. On the rivers and streams there were more than 200 saw mills when the rebellion broke out, and many more might be erected. The rivers abound with salmon and various other kinds of fish; several of which rivers are navigable 50 or 60 miles for ships of 300 tons, and much further for small craft. There are, on the sea-coast from Falmouth to Passamaquodie, which is about 70 leagues, more than twenty harbours; many of them are very large, with deep water and good bottom, and are not incommoded with ice in the winter season, viz.: Falmouth, Sheepscut, Townsend, George Islands, Penobscot, Algemogin, Bass, Cranberry Island, Frenchman's Bay, Gooldsborough, Machias, Narraguagus,¶ and East Passomaquodie. In each of these harbours ships of the largest size may ride in safety in the most violent winds. In the harbour of

† When full grown the carcass weighs from 600 to 800 lbs.
‡ For this article Britain has hitherto been obliged to the Northern Powers, Russia in particular.
¶ Falmouth consisted of what is now Portland, Westbrook and Falmouth, and the harbor is Portland harbor.
Townsend was what is now Boothbay.
Cranberry Islands lie on the outside of Mount Desert Island.
Narraguagus Bay is at Millbridge.

Majabigwaduce is a large sandy beach; the tide flows from 15 to 18 feet, and a dock-yard may be erected there at a small expence, for the collection of masts, lumber, etc., and to heave down the largest men of war. Near the entrance of the harbour is good fishing ground, where cod, shell and several other kinds of fish are taken in plenty.

In October, 1772, there were in this District, 42 towns and 2638 families,§ who have since greatly increased, at least in the proportion of one-fourth, which is 659 families, making in the whole 3297 families. Reckoning these, five souls to each family (which is a moderate computation) there are now 16,485 souls. To this New Country the Loyalists resort with their families (last summer, particularly, a great number of families were preparing to remove thither) from the New England Provinces, and find an asylum from the tyranny of Congress and their tax-gatherers, as well as daily employment in fishing, lumbering, clearing and preparing land for their subsistence; and there they continue, in full hope and pleasing expectation, that they may soon re-enjoy the liberties and privileges which would be best secured to them by laws, and under a form of government, modelled after the British Constitution; and that they may be covered in their possessions, agreeably to the petition to the Throne, in 1773; which was renewed last year.

Should this District be severed from the Province of Massachusetts Bay, and erected into a Province under the authority of the Crown, and the inhabitants *quieted* in their *possessions,* it would be settled with amazing rapidity; the Royal Navy, West India Islands, and other parts of His Majesty's Dominion, well and plentifully served for centuries to come from this District, with every article above mentioned without being obliged to other Powers for the same; and the profits of the whole would fall into the lap of Great Britain in return for her manufactures. Roads

§ As appears by a list then taken by a respectable person.

A JOURNAL OF THE SIEGE OF PENOBSCOT

would moreover be opened for communication with other His Majesty's Provinces, which migh be travelled in a short time by the following routes:

Distance from Quebeck.

	MILES
To Passadonkeeg, Indian Old Town, on Penobscot River	65
Sawedabscook	35
Fort Halifax on Kennebeck River	19
* Pownalborough	33
Falmouth	54
Portsmouth	53
Boston	65
	324

Distance from Annapolis, Nova Scotia.

	MILES
To St. John's, 16 leagues	48
Penobscot River	55
Fort Halifax	19
Boston	205
	327

N. B. From Boston to Fort Halifax is a good Cart Road.

(P. 35) Fort Pownall was built by Governor Thomas Pownall and was completed in July, 1759. It was on Fort Point in what is now Stockton, Maine, at the head of Penobscot Bay, fourteen miles from Belfast. It was dismantled in 1776 by Captain Henry Mowat, and in 1779 the British burned the buildings and leveled the earthworks to make it useless.

* Pownalborough consisted of what is now Dresden, Alna, Perkins and Wiscasset, Maine, and was the shire town of Lincoln County.

CAPTAIN HENRY MOWAT'S ACCOUNT

(In the catalogue of a London bookseller, in 1843, appeared for sale a manuscript relating to the services of Capt. Henry Mowat in America. It was disposed of, to whom was unknown. The title was " A relation of the services in which Captain Henry Mowat was engaged in America, from 1759 to the end of the American War in 1783." Search was instituted by Maine historians for the manuscript. Judge Joseph Williamson, of Belfast, Maine, advertised abroad, in 1887, " I will pay five pounds for evidence of the existence of the manuscript." On November 20, 1890, it was received by Hon. James P. Baxter, of Portland, from Edinburgh, and was published in part, with its history, in the *Collections* of the Maine Historical Society, Series II, Vol. 2, page 345. The original manuscript of fifty-nine pages is now in the possession of that society. The following is the part relating to the occupancy of the Penobscot by the British during the Revolution; beginning with the middle of page 7 and ending near the bottom of page 21. Punctuation, spelling and capitalization are as in the original.)

THE *Albany* at last was called to New York in the beginning of 1779—orders had not long before arrived from Britain for taking post in Penobscot Bay, and Capt. Mowat's experience of the New England Coast being well known to Sir Henry Clinton on former occasions, he was proposed by his Excellency approved by Admiral Gambier as the fittest to command the naval part of the Force. The Admiral desiring to know the force necessary for the Service, was answered it should be Superior to any the Enemy at Boston could readily collect on such Emergency. It was accordingly settled it should be so, and that Captain Mowat should have a ship equal to the Importance of the object.

In the meantime the Store of Powder in the Garrison at Halifax being totally exhausted, Captain Mowat received on board the *Albany* and proceeded with an ample Supply, the orders and

Every equipment for the Expedition, being intended to follow: but he had no sooner landed the Powder, than he was ordered by Sir George Collier to the Bay of Fundy, and Sir George repaired soon after to New York where he was left the Senior Officer on the American Station.

On this change taking place, Captain Mowat, from reasons otherwise foreign to this Narrative, Considered it Necessary to urge what he had formerly represented to Admiral Gambier, and he wrote to New York from the Bay of Fundy, that if the *Albany* were to be the leading Ship, it would by no means be safe to trust the Expedition with one of her class, unless a Sufficient force should cruize between it & the enemy, until the post should be established.

This representation appears to have had no effect, for the orders for the *Albany* alone soon after arrived at Halifax, and were delivered by Capt. Gaylor of the *Romulus* to General McLean until the *Albany* should arrive.

Thus, if the *Albany* had happened to lead the Expedition according to the order, the whole must have been intercepted as we shall shortly see, & carried to Boston for a mere Novice might have conceived at once She was not fit to conduct it safely. The Consequences, which must be estimated according to the view & State of affairs at that time in America, Would have been tremendous. It would have been equivalent to a Second Burgoynade before there were time for repairing, or forgetting, the first: an immense Encouragement for the Americans, who were tiring of the length of the war, to exert their remaining resources, for the Opposition to exercise their clamor, and a proportional depression of the Spirits of the Loyalists. To the Southward we had but a slender footing in Georgia against such a disaster, the reinforcements not arrived as yet And the Army there inactive for Security. To the Northward Canada was not so strong as it had been rendered in the Succeeding Year, And Nova Scotia at least, lying contiguous to the territory of Penobscot, would have been overwhelmed, for by this detachment the Garrison of Halifax had been by the one-half reduced. This disposition of the Service must appear the more strange as we know Sir George Collier was by no means ignorant of the rebel force in the New England Ports.

But the dire Event was prevented by a mere accident & that the most fortunate in the World; for the Dispatch, forwarded by General McLean, did not reach the Bay of Fundy where Capt. Mowat was stationed, nor did he in Consequence get round to Halifax, until the latest moment having elapsed the General put the order into the hands of Captain Barclay* of the *Blonde* Frigate, then Senior officer of the Navy there, who immediately put the *North* & *Nautilus* sloops of war under orders to proceed with himself And they were on the point of sailing when the *Albany* arrived. However this did not alter Captain Barclay's judicious determination. They proceeded, had a long passage As might be expected at the Season, and at last arrived at Penobscot: The Rebel frigates, *Boston* & *Providence,* who were cruizing on the Coast of Nova Scotia westward of Halifax, finding the Convoy Superior to what they expected, did not think proper to attack it.

In a few days after the troops were landed, the *Blonde* departed, leaving Captain Mowat under a copy of Sir George Collier's original orders, with directions for the *North* and *Nautilus* & all the transports to return to Halifax. Now soon the stores were landed for Captain Barclay had brought the Sloops of War there without Sir George Collier's orders, Captain Mowat finding the wretched *Albany* was to be left thus alone, to lie in an open har-

*Andrew Barklay, the captain of the frigate *Blonde,* called by one who saw her, "a beautiful ship," was a Loyalist from Boston. He was a protestor against the Whigs in 1774. After peace was declared, accompanied by his family of ten persons and by four servants, he left New York for Shelburne, Nova Scotia, where the Crown granted him fifty acres of land, one town and one water lot. He was living there in 1805.

bour distant from every Aid, and in the Jaws of the most powerful of the rebellious Colonies, to co-operate with about 700 troops in a fort not yet begun to be erected, was convinced it would be for the good of His Majesty's Service to use the utmost Latitude, the order would admit of, to postpone the departure of the Ships, from the following view of the Situation of the Armament.

The Bay of the Penobscot is spacious and capable of containing all the Navy in the World. In a corner of it about fourteen leagues distant from the open Sea, near the Embrochure (*sic*) of Penobscot River is the Harbour of Magebigwaduce. This Harbour is formed on the one Side by the Mainland, and along the entire other side of it Stretches the Peninsula of Magebigwaduce. Cross[1] —now Nautilus Island—is at the entrance of the Harbor. The Peninsula of Magebigwaduce is a high Ridge of land at that time much encumbered with wood. To its summit, where the fort was ordered to be erected there is an ascent of more than a quarter of a mile from the nearest shore of the harbour.

The Provisions, Artillery and Engineer Stores and the equipage of the troops, being landed on the Beach, must be carried to the Ground of the fort chiefly by the labor of the men against the ascent, there being only a Couple of small teams to Assist in it. The ground & all the Avenues to it, was to be examined, cleared from wood, and at the same time guarded. Materials were to be collected & prepared, And the defences, as well as every convenience of the fort, were to be reared. Let any one conversant in Matters of this Nature, reflect what a work it was for 700 men, And he will also readily allow, that in the Course of it they could not possibly, whether from fatigue, or in point of Necessary Preparation be in Condition of repelling any powerful attack. That, as appears also

[1] Nautilus or Cross Island, sometimes called Banks' Island, for its owner, is southeast of Castine in Penobscot Bay and was named for the sloop of war *Nautilus*.

from the rebel General Lovel's letter, everything depended on our Men of War being able to prevent the Enemy from entering the Harbour, which was not liable to be commanded or protected by the Guns of the Fort. That the Harbour once forced, a Superior Number of the Enemy might land on the most convenient parts of the Peninsula, cut off the communication of our Troops with that considerable part of the Necessary Stores, which to the last while the fort was erecting, must unavoidably be left on the Beach, force them to retire within the unfinished Breastwork, where Surrounded without cover, Comfort or defence, they could have no alternative but to yield Prisoners of War in a few days, or to risk an action against thrice their number on ground from its Nature more favorable to the Enemy's mode of fighting than for theirs. It is altogether Superfluous to comment any farther on the orders by which a harbour, of this Importance must be left to the sole protection of the *Albany* Sloop, carrying ten Six and Six four pounders.

The *Blonde* Frigate had not been many days departed, when Captain Mowat having taken Measures for procuring the best information from Boston, concluded that the Post would soon be attacked, and he proposed to General McLean to give his concurrence for detaining the *North* & *Nautilus,* as well as the Transports, judging the General's Consent to be eligible, because otherwise he would be liable to Account for acting contrary to the orders left with him.

The General equally confident in the Intelligence, gave his Concurrence, and accordingly in the fifth week from the Arrival of the Royal Armament at Penobscot, the Rebel fleet appeared in the Bay, consisting of eighteen vessels of war as per the margin,** besides Transports having on board all necessary Stores and between two and three thousand Land forces.

At that time a great portion of the stores had not as yet been

** No list attached.

carried up to the fort. Its Scite was lower by several feet, than a piece of ground at the distance of six hundred yards. The Parapet, fronting this higher ground was scarcely four feet high. All the other parts of the Parapet, paralell to the Harbour of Magebagwaduce and in the rear, were not three feet high. The two Bastions to the harbour were quite open. The troops were encamped on the area, which might be about the Space of an Acre, there had been a Shade erected for the Provisions. The Powder was lodged in covered holes dug in the proposed *Glacis*: There was but a Single Gun Mounted, & that a Six Pounder.

The Naval force in Magebagwaduce Harbour were the *Albany, North* & *Nautilus,* Sloops of War, Commanded by Captains Mowat, Selby and Farnham, and four Transports.

In this force and State of Preparation, one may easier conceive than describe the anxiety & hopes of all concerned on the appearance of so formidable an Armament.

The enemy came up, and paraded before the entrance of the harbour, in perfect confidence of entering it without difficulty, which would have been the case had the *Albany* been alone, and then everything would have been over at once; but there was such an excellent Disposition made of the Sloops of War & Transports in the entrance of the Harbour, as baffled every attempt of the Enemy to force it for three days—then they prepared to land their troops on a Bluff of the Peninsula without the harbour, where the General could place pickets communicating with the Main body in the fort, to watch & to oppose, the debarkation.

These three or four days of Embarrassment on the part of the rebels gave our troops time to do something more to the Fort, to carry up the most necessary Stores, to mount several guns, and in short to devote every Endeavor to the present Exigency. The Enemy, having failed in their attempts on the harbour, effected at last a landing on the bluff, and by superior numbers forced the Pickets into the Fort, took possession of the high ground, above mentioned, within six hundred yards thereof & immediately erected their Batteries and Lines.

In this Position both Parties continued firing at one another during the whole Siege. Our Troops, tho' extremely harassed, were daily getting into a better Situation, with the Assistance of the Seamen, and the Requisites which the Men of War furnished, as well as their own Stores. Secure on the Flanks & in the rear while our Ships maintained the Harbour, they had only to exert their chief attention & Efforts on the side fronting the Enemies Lines, which effectually deterred the latter from advancing in that direction.

They had erected Batteries on Nautilus Island, & in the rear of the harbour, all within point blanc shot shot of any position, in which the ships could be placed, but the proper choice of different stations on every emergency eluded their utmost efforts to enter it.

Thus both sides were employed, ashore & afloat, for 21 Days, in a variety of Manouveres, which are in part described in a Journal kept by an officer on shore & published by J. C. Esq.

In the Mean time Intelligence having reached New York, that Penobscot was attacked, Sir George Collier Sailed to its relief, with the *Raisonable* Ship of the Line, *Blonde, Virginia, Carmilla, Galatea,* &c. They were perceived off Penobscot Bay by the rebel look-out vessel in the Evening. In the course of the night they embarked their Troops, &c., and in the Morning early their fleet was seen under Sail; but the wind failing them to get round the upper end of Long Island, they had no alternative but to run up Penobscot River. These Manouvres were a proof that the Strange Ships sailing up the Bay were a relief and the three Sloops of

War being employed from daylight in embarking the part of their Guns that were ashore on the Batteries, &c., &c., were able to join in the center of the King's Ships: during the pursuit one of the rebel vessels struck, after a few shots, to the *Blonde* & *Virginia*: Another ran ashore at the same time some distance below the mouth of the River, and was some time after taken possession of by the *Raisonable,* which brought up the rear: All the rest, with the advantage of good pilots & of a whole flood tide which happened in the night, got such a distance up the River, as afforded time for destroying them, And the crews made the best of their way to New England, thro' the woods, in the utmost distress.

Thus ended the attack on Penobscot.—It was positively the severest blow received by the American Naval force during the War. The trade to Canada, which was intended, after the expected reduction of the Post of Penobscot, to be intercepted by this very armament, went safe that Season: The New England Provinces did not for the remaining period of the contest recover the loss of Ships, and the Expence of fitting out the Expedition: Every thought of attempting Canada, & Nova Scotia, was thenceforth laid aside, and the trade & Transports from the Banks of Newfoundland along the Coast of Nova Scotia, &c: enjoyed unusual Security.

After all was over, it was natural to be expected, that Sir George Collier would have been Supremely happy to have represented this important Service in its proper colors, and that Capt. Mowat would, according to the Custom of the Service, have been sent home with the Account: But in answer to the Claim, Sir George expressed the utmost regret, that he could not spare a Ship from the Station: assured that if he intended to send an officer to England Capt. Mowat would certainly be the person; that he only meant to transmit the Despatches by New York, in which he pledged his word, as he held it to be no more than his duty, that the

Services of the Sloops of War would be represented in the most honorable Manner to the Admiralty—

On the next day & before there was time to attend to writing the Official Account of the Siege, he put the *Albany* under orders to proceed up Penobscot River to the Rebel Wrecks, observing it would be some time before he would leave the Bay—This done he departed abruptly for New York, and had no sooner gone out to Sea, than the *Greyhound's* Signal was made to part Company, And she proceeded directly to England with his Account.

Her destination had been Kept a Secret from everyone, General McLean excepted, who in his publick Letter Acknowledges having been privately informed. This is the Manner, in which Captain Mowat was prevented Sending an Official Account of the Siege, And, Notwithstanding Sir George Collier having solemnly pledged himself as above, we See his account to the Admiralty confined to the Merit which we will readily allow him of sailing from New York to the relief with a Squadron Which the United Naval force of All America was incompetent to resist even in a Crescent & to a description of the Disposition & destruction of the Rebel Ships, which however could not be discerned by any one from on board the *Raisonable*: The Service of the three Sloops of War during the Siege were totally omitted & their Captains not even named.

When Admiral Arbuthnot's arrival had put an end to Sir George Collier's Command, Captain Mowat hoped some Justice would have been done him for the Service performed at Penobscot, at least so far as the laying a fair representation of it before the Admiralty, but there was not the least notice taken of him, and he was left at Magebigwaduce under a continuation of the distress of seeing also, that every Promotion, made by this Admiral, was without a single exception, of officers Junior to him: Among these an Officer, who had received his first Commission into the *Albany* when Captain Mowat was appointed to her, was made Post Captain: It is not from any individious (sic) Motive this Instance is given on Captain's Mowat's part: None can be more happy in the good fortune of an Officer, with whose great Merit he has had opportunities of being well Acquainted: but it is a Contrast to the glaring Injustice himself has Met with.

Henry Mowat was born in Scotland in 1734. He was the son of Capt. Patrick Mowat of H. M. S. *Dolphin*. After an experience of six years he was commissioned as lieutenant of the *Baltimore* in 1756. The certificate of his " passing " in the Admiralty records sets forth " He produceth records kept by himself in the *Chesterfield* and *Ramlis* (Ramillies) (as midshipman) and certificates from Captains Ogle and Hobbs of the *Dilligence*, etc.; he can splice, knot, reef a sail, etc., and is qualified to do the duty of an able seaman and midshipman." In 1762, he was promoted to be a commander and served as such on the *Canceaux* twelve years. It was during this time that he destroyed Falmouth Neck, now Portland. This event occurred October 18, 1775, and for it he was denounced by our forefathers and Washington wrote of his conduct, " I know not how sufficiently to detest it." Mowat was then forty-one years old. He had been captured at Falmouth Neck, the May before, and was released on his promise to return the next morning, which promise he did not keep. His next vessel, the sloop *Albany*, was the flag-ship of the squadron at Penobscot. He served his King forty-four years, about thirty of which were on our coast. On board his ship, the *Assistance*, about five miles from Cape Henry, Va., April 14, 1798, he was stricken with apoplexy, died aged sixty-four years, and was buried in St. John's church yard, at Hampton, Va. He left a son, John Alexander, who entered the navy in 1804.

NATHAN GOOLD.

Eyewitness Accounts of the American Revolution

The Penobscot Expedition

The New York Times & Arno Press

Reprint Edition 1971 by Arno Press Inc.

*

LC# 78-140857
ISBN 0-405-01226-8

*

Eyewitness Accounts of the American Revolution, Series III
ISBN for complete set: 0-405-01187-3

*

Manufactured in the United States of America

EDITOR'S PREFACE

HEN we published our No. 11, on the Penobscot Expedition, we did not know of the existence of the present rare report of the Massachusetts Committee of Investigation or we would have incorporated it with the other.

The history of all wars where the Army and Navy were to co-operate is full of accounts of failures due to the lack of such co-operation.

The story of Penobscot is but one of such. Saltonstall must have had strong political influence, to have escaped a more serious punishment than dismissal from the Continental Navy (October 7, 1779). He afterward commanded a privateer which made some good captures, and died in 1796.

THE PROCEEDINGS

OF THE

GENERAL ASSEMBLY

AND OF THE

COUNCIL,

OF THE

STATE OF MASSACHUSETTS-BAY,

RELATING TO THE

Penobscot EXPEDITION:

AND THE

ORDERS of the CONTINENTAL NAVY-BOARD

TO THE

COMMANDER of the NAVAL FORCES.

TOGETHER

With the REPORT of a COMMITTEE
Appointed to enquire into the CAUSE of the
FAILURE of the said EXPEDITION.

PUBLISHED BY ORDER OF THE GENERAL ASSEMBLY

BOSTON:

PRINTED BY J. GILL, PRINTER TO THE GENERAL ASSEMBLY.

1780.

STATE of MASSACHUSETTS-BAY

IN THE HOUSE OF REPRESENTATIVES,
December 30, 1779.

RESOLVED, That it appears to this Court, upon a full enquiry into the grounds and reasons of the failure of the late Expedition to *Penobscot*, that the principal causes of the failure aforesaid are clearly pointed out in the several questions and answers contained in the report of the Committee of both Houses on the 7th of *October* last, relative to this matter, which appears to be fully supported by the depositions accompanying the same: And in order that the public may be satisfied with respect to the conduct of said expedition,

RESOLVED, That the report of the Committee of Enquiry, of the 7th *October* last, and the resolves, and a letter of the General Court to MESHECH WEARE, Esq; and also the orders and letters of the Council, relative to this Expedition, hereafter enumerated; together with the orders given by the Navy-Board to the Commander of the Naval Forces, be published in a pamphlet.

Sent up for concurrence.

JOHN HANCOCK, Speaker.

IN C O U N C I L, *December* 30, 1779.

R E A D and concurred.

JOHN AVERY, D. Secr'y.

Consented to by the major part of the Council.

The papers referred to above, to be published, are as follows, viz.

Resolve for raising 1200 men in the counties of *Lincoln* and *Cumberland*, for the *Penobscot* expedition, and making provision for said troops, and appointing General Lovell to the command; passed *June 26, 1779.*

WHEREAS this Court, in order to dislodge the enemy now landed on Penobscot, *have by their resolve of the 24th instant directed the Board of War to equip a fleet for that purpose, and as it will be necessary to have a land force to co-operate therewith:*

Resolved, That the Council of this State be and hereby are requested to issue orders to the Brigadier of the county of *Cumberland,* to detach from his brigade six hundred men immediately, to be formed into one regiment with proper officers, equipped according to the militia act, to march immediately to *Penobscot,* to be under the command of the Brigadier hereinafter appointed, to serve for two months after they shall arrive at *Penobscot,* unless sooner discharged, and that the said Council be and hereby are requested to issue orders to the Brigadier of the county of *Lincoln* to detach from his brigade a like number of men, formed, equipped and marched as aforesaid, said regiments to be upon such an establishment as this Court shall hereafter make; and the men heretofore ordered from the aforesaid brigades to fill up the Continental battalions shall be considered as part of said detachments, and be marched to *Penobscot,* or such other place as the Commanding Officer shall direct; and in case the expedition is carried on, the said counties of *Cumberland* and *Lincoln* shall be excused from raising their proportion of men to fill up the Continental army for nine months.

And it is further *Resolved,* That the Council be and hereby are requested to order the Board of War immediately to prepare and send on to *Penobscot,* to such place as the Council shall order, for the use of said detachment, nine tons of flour or bread, nine tons of rice, eighteen tons of salt beef, six hundred gallons of rum, six hundred gallons of molasses, five hundred stand of fire-arms, fifty-thousand small-arm cartridges, two eighteen pound cannon, two hundred rounds of cartridges and shot for ditto, three cannon (nine pounders) with three hundred rounds of cartridges for ditto, four field-pieces, (four pounders) and four hundred rounds of cartridges for ditto, one howizer, and shot or shells proper therefor, one hundred rounds, six barrels of gun-powder, and such number of camp kettles, spades, shovels, pick-axes and chopping-axes, as the Commanding-Officer herein after appointed may think proper for said expedition.

And it is further *Resolved*, That the Council be and they are hereby requested to order Col. *Revere*, with one hundred of the train under his command, to *Penobscot*, on said expedition; and the said Col. *Revere* is hereby appointed to command the ordnance during said expedition, under the direction of the Commander in Chief there.

And be it further *Resolved*, That *Solomon Lovell*, Esq; Brigadier-General, be and he is hereby appointed to command the above-said detachments destined to *Penobscot* aforesaid, and advise with the Commander of the fleet destined there, to guide and direct the land movements in said expedition, to the utter expulsion of the enemy from this State, and the Council are requested to commission him accordingly.

And it is hereby *Resolved*, That the Council of this State shall from time to time give such orders to said Commander, and further reinforce and supply by land or sea as to them may appear reasonable to answer the purpose designed.

Resolve requesting the Council to detach 300 men from the county of York, *for the* Penobscot *expedition, and directing the Board of War to provide for the armed vessels at* Newbury-Port, *and impowering the Council to impress vessels; passed* June 29, 1779.

*R*ESOLVED, That the Council be requested to issue their orders to the Brigadier or Commanding-Officer of the county of *York*, to detach from his brigade three hundred men, and form them into companies with proper officers, equipped according to the militia law of this State, and hold them in readiness to march to *Penobscot* under the command of General *Lovell*, to attack the enemy there; to serve for the term of two months, unless sooner discharged.

Resolved, That the Board of War be directed immediately to send to *Newbury-Port*, a quantity of provisions to victual for a two months' cruize, one ship of twenty-four guns, one of twenty, two of sixteen guns, which the merchants there have agreed to man for the *Penobscot* expedition: And that the said Board of War take measures immediately to compleat the crews of the Continental vessels now in this harbour, for the aforesaid expedition, to continue in that service only for the term of two months, unless sooner discharged; and that the said Board send to *Salem* and procure two twenty gun ships or more, for said expedition immediately.

Resolved, That the Council be and hereby are requested to write to the Continental Navy-Board, requesting them to aid the *Penobscot* expedition with the Continental vessels now in this harbour, and fit them immediately therefor.

Resolved, That the Council be and hereby are impowered to hire or impress any vessel or vessels, other than the Continental or those belonging to this State, should the exigencies of the State require it, and forward the *Penobscot* expedition as soon as possible. Also;

Resolved, That the Council be and hereby are impowered to take such measures as they shall judge necessary to carry into effect the expedition aforesaid, and to draw on the treasury for any sum not exceeding *fifty thousand pounds* for this purpose.

A letter from the honorable General Assembly of the State of Massachusetts-Bay *to the Hon.* MESHECH WEARE, *Esq., President of the honorable Council of the State of* New-Hampshire, *dated June 29, 1779.*

SIR,

I HAVE the honor to acquaint you, by order of the General Assembly, of the information we have received of the enemy's landing a detachment of their troops at Penobscot and of the measures the General Assembly have taken to expel them from that part of this State; and to request the vigorous co-operation of the State of New-Hampshire with us, in a measure so important to the interest of both states.

The inclosed resolutions will give you the fullest information upon the subject and it is desired that they may be laid before your General Assembly, if fitting, to the end that they may seasonably afford such assistance as they may judge reasonable.

(signed)   JEREMIAH POWELL, President
Honorable Meshech Weare, *Esq.*
President of the State of New-Hampshire

To be communicated to the Hon. General Assembly of said State or in its recess to the Hon. Council thereof.

Council's Order on the Board of War, dated July 1, 1779.

ORDERED, That the Board of War be and hereby are directed to take up three hundred tons of shipping, upon the best terms they can, and send them to the town of *Wells*, in the County of *York*, in order to transport the three hundred men ordered to be detached from that county to *Penobscot*; and they are also directed to cause provisions sufficient to victual the three hundred men aforesaid, one month, to be conveyed in as secret a manner as possible to *Joshua Bragdon*, at the town aforesaid—and they are further directed to take up six hundred tons of shipping, upon the best terms they can, and send them to *Falmouth* in the county of *Cumberland*, in order to transport the six hundred men ordered to be detached from that county to *Penobscot;* and also to cause provisions sufficient to victual the six hundred men aforementioned one month, to be conveyed in the most secret manner to

Capt. *Joseph Noyes* at *Falmouth*.—And they are further directed to take up six hundred tons of shipping, upon the best terms they can, and send them in company with the fleet that may sail from *Nantasket* to *Townsend*, in the County of Lincoln in order to transport the six hundred men ordered to be detached from that County to *Penobscot*.

And it is further *Ordered*, That *Townsend* in the province of *Main* be and hereby is assigned as a place of general rendezvous for the land and naval force destined to attack the enemy at *Penobscot*.

And it is further *Ordered*, That the Board of War be and hereby is directed to provide a Doctor's box, under the direction of Dr. *Joseph Gardner*, for the use of the troops raised for the Penobscot expedition.

Council's Order to General Lovell, *dated* July 1, 1779.

ORDERED, That Brigadier-General *Lovell*, appointed to command the troops ot be raised for the present expedition to the Eastward be, and hereby is directed to send three suitable persons, who may attend him thro' the campaign immediately to the Southward, one to *Wells*, in the County of *York*, one to *Falmouth*, in the county of *Cumberland*, and one to *Broad Bay*, in the County of *Lincoln*, in order to expedite the raising the men aforesaid, and to direct them to march to the several places of rendezvous, appointed in the several counties abovementioned, at such time as he shall judge proper, upon consulting with the commander of the fleet destined upon the Expedition aforesaid.

Council's Order to General Lovell, *dated* July 2, 1779.

SIR,

YOU being appointed by the General. Court of this State, to the command of the land forces, raised and to be raised for the purpose of dislodging the enemies of this State, who have taken post at *Penobscot*: You will therefore immediately prepare for and set out on your journey to the Eastern part of this State. When you arrive there you will without loss of time cause the troops ordered to be raised in that quarter, to assemble at the place appointed for the place of general rendezvous; and when they arrive there, you will loose no time, but cause them to embark on board the transports which are provided for the purpose of transporting the troops to *Penobscot*; and when you arrive at *Penobscot*, you will consult such measures as shall appear to you most likely to effect the salutary purpose designed by this State in undertaking the expedition aforesaid. You will at all times study to promote the greatest harmony, peace and concord, between the land and sea forces engaged in the enterprize aforesaid. You will in all your operations consult with the Commander of the fleet, that the naval force may co-operate with the troops under your command, in endeavoring to captivate, kill or destroy the whole force of the enemy there, both by sea and land. And as there is good reason to believe that some of the principal men at *Majorbagwayduce*, requested the enemy to come there and take possession, you will be particularly careful not to let any of them escape, but to secure them that they may receive a just reward for their evil-doings. You will be peculiarly careful to forward to the Council intelligence from time to time, of your movements. If you shall find that you stand in need of a reinforcement to enable you to subdue the post of the enemy at *Penobscot*, you will call upon the militia in the lower counties in this State, for such reinforcement as you shall judge adequate.

We now commend you to the Supreme Being, sincerely praying Him to preserve you and the forces under your command in health and safety, and return you crowned with victory and laurels.

In the name and behalf of the Council,
JEREMIAH POWELL, President.

P. S. In case the enemy should leave *Penobscot* and invade any other place or places in the counties of *York*, *Cumberland* or *Lincoln* in this State, you are hereby directed to pursue them with the force under your command, and dislodge them; and in case the enemy upon your arrival should have left *Penobscot* and returned to *Halifax*, you may then as soon as you may think it safe and convenient, dismiss the militia, or such part of them as you think best, and send them by the transports to such ports as may be most contiguous to their respective homes.

Council's Order on the Board of War, dated July 2, 1779.

ORDERED, That the Board of War be and they hereby are directed to take two hundred barrels of unappropriated powder at Castle Island, and deliver the same to Col. *William Burbeck*, for the purpose of preparing the ammunition for the intended expedition; and to replace the said quantity of powder as soon as may be.

Council's Order to the Sheriff of the county of Suffolk, *to press the ship* General Putnam, *dated* July 2, 1779.

WHEREAS *it appears to this Board that it is absolutely necessary to compleat a sufficient naval force for the* Penobscot *expedition, that the ship* General Putnam *now in this harbour, should be taken in to that service immediately, and the owners thereof being at a distance:*

Therefore *Ordered*, That the Sheriff of the county of *Suffolk*, be and he hereby is impowered and directed to impress the ship *General Putnam*, with her tackle and appurtenances, and deliver her to the Board of War, to fit her immediately for a two month's cruize, to sail on an expedition to *Penobscot*, to dispossess the enemy of the United States there, and this shall be your sufficient warrant.— Hereof fail not, and make due return of this warrant, with your doings thereon, forthwith.

In the name and behalf of the Council,

JEREMIAH POWELL, President

JOHN AVERY, D. Secr'y.

Council's Order to the Sheriff of *Essex*, to impress vessels, dated
July 3, 1779.

To the Sheriff of the county of Essex, his under Sheriff or Deputy,
Greeting.

*W*HEREAS *it appears to this Board that it is absolutely necessary to compleat a sufficient naval force for the* Penobscot *expedition, that three ships now in the harbour of* Salem, *viz.* The ships Hector, Black Prince *and* Hunter, *should be taken into that service immediately: And whereas the owners and commanders thereof have refused to hire the said ships into the service of this State to be employed in the proposed expedition to* Penobscot, *upon the terms mentioned in the resolutions of the General Assembly of this State, of the 29th day of* June *last:*

YOU, and each of you, are hereby impowered and commanded to impress the said three ships, with their tackles and appurtenances, and deliver them to the Board of War, to fit them immediately for a two month's cruize, to sail on an expedition to *Penobscot,* to dispossess the enemies of the United States there: And this shall be your sufficient warrant.—Hereof fail not, and make due return of this warrant, with your doings thereon, forthwith.

GIVEN at the Council Chamber in Boston, *this third day of* July, *in the year of our Lord* One thousand seven hundred and seventy-nine, *and in the third year of the Independence of the United States of America.*

In the name and behalf of the Council,
JEREMIAH POWELL, President.

JOHN AVERY, D. Secr'y.

Council's Order for pressing men, dated *July* 3, 1779.
To the Sheriff of the county of   his Under-Sheriff or Deputy,
Greeting.

*W*HEREAS *the General Assembly by their resolution of the 30th day of* June *last, did impower the Council in case the vessels designed for the expedition to* Penobscot *cannot be reasonably manned in the usual way (which now appears to the Council)* to issue *press-warrants to such officers as they shall judge proper for the purpose of procuring men for said vessels for a term of time not exceeding two months:*

YOU, and each of you, are hereby authorized and commanded, taking with you such assistance as you judge proper, forthwith to take seize and impress any able-bodied seaman or mariner which you shall find in your precinct (Captains or masters of any ships or vessels excepted) to serve on board any of the vessels entered into the service of this State, to be employed in the proposed expedition to *Penobscot*, for and during the said term of two months from the date of said resolution, unless sooner duly discharged; and for the more effectual execution of this warrant, You are hereby authorized to enter on board and search any ship or vessel, or to break open and search any dwelling-house or other building in which you shall suspect any such seamen or mariners to be concealed, first demanding peaceable entrance thereinto of any person within such dwelling-house or other building for the purpose of executing this warrant, and it being refused or not given you: And all such able-bodied seamen or mariners as you shall find within your district, and shall impress as aforesaid, you are to deliver over to   , who is hereby authorised and directed to retain them in his custody until they shall be, by order of Council, properly assigned to and among the vessels aforesaid.

GIVEN at the **Council-Chamber**, *under our hands and the seal of the said State*, at **Boston**, *this third day of* **July**, *A. D.* **One thousand seven hundred and seventy-nine**, *and in the third year of the Independence of the United States of* **America**.

Signed by the major part of the Council,

JOHN AVERY, Dep. Sec'ry.

PROCEEDINGS OF THE GENERAL ASSEMBLY 53

Council's Order to the Board of War to provide provisions, dated July 3, 1779.

ORDERED, That the Board of War be, and they hereby are directed to procure three hundred and fifty barrels of flour, one hundred and sixteen barrels of pork, one hundred and sixty-five barrels of beef, eleven tierces of rice, three hundred and fifty bushels of pease, five hundred and fifty-two gallons of molasses, two thousand one hundred and seventy-six pounds of soap, and seven hundred and sixty-eight pounds of candles, being a deficient quantity in the schedule hereunto annexed, and ship the same on board the transports for the intended expedition to *Penobscot*.

The Schedule referred to in the foregoing, *viz*

Should be.		Already shipped.		Short.	
Flour 89,600 lb.	Flour 448 bbs.	6000	90 bbs.	358 bbs.	N.B. 6 tons bread as 60 bbs. flour
Pork 25,600 lb.	Pork 116 bbs.	—	—	116 bbs.	
Beef 80,000 lb.	Beef. 333bbs.	40,320 lb.	168 bbs.	165 bbs.	
Rice 22,400 lb.	45 tierces	17,000 lb.	34 tierces.	11 tierces.	
Pease. 350 bu.	—	—	—	350 bu.	
Molasses 1,152 gal's	—	600 gal's.	—	552 gall's.	N. B. 6 lb. to 100 men week for guards
Soap. 2,176 lb.	—	—	—	2,176 lb.	
Candles. 768 lb.	—	—	—	768 lbs.	
Vinegar					

The above is calculated for 1,600 men for eight weeks.

WAR-OFFICE, *July* 3, 1779.

THIS Schedule has been laid before us by Mr. *Lucas*, the Commissary appointed by your Honors for this expedition, and considerably exceeds the quantity heretofore directed: We shall fulfil any orders your Honors give hereon.

SAM. PH. SAVAGE.

Council's Order to the Board of War, of **August 8, 1779.**

*O*RDERED, That the Board of War be and they hereby are directed immediately to procure one hundred barrels of bread, eight hundred gallons of rum, two hundred stand of arms compleat, four hundred cartridge-boxes, and fifteen barrels of powder, for the troops upon the expedition to *Penobscot.*

Council's Letter to the Navy-Board, dated **June 30, 1779.**

GENTLEMEN,

THE General Assembly of this State have determined on an expedition to *Penobscot*, to dislodge the enemy of the United States lately entered there, who are said to be committing hostilities on the good people of this State, and *vi et armis* fortifying themselves at *Majorbagwayduce*; and as they are supported by a considerable naval force, to effect our design it will be expedient to send there to aid our land operations, a superior naval force.—Therefore, Gentlemen, in consequence of a resolve of the General Assembly, a copy of which is here inclosed, we write you in the most pressing manner, requesting you to aid our designs by adding to the naval force of this State, now with all possible speed preparing for an expedition to *Penobscot*, the Continental frigate now in this harbour, and the other armed Continental vessels here; by which addition we shall have a force superior to the enemy there, and may resonably promise ourselves success.

Gentlemen, You will on receipt hereof, acquaint this Board of your determinations on this important matter, and of the naval force you can aid us with, and how soon such force can be made ready.

You may be assured that should you need the assistance of this

PROCEEDINGS OF THE GENERAL ASSEMBLY 55

State in manning the said ships speedily, this Board will give you all the aid in their power to effect so valuable a purpose.

In the name and behalf of the Council,
I am, Gentlemen,
Your humble servant,

Hon. NAVY-BOARD.   J. POWELL, President.

Council's Letter to the Navy-Board, dated July 2, 1779.

GENTLEMEN,

THE Commander of the Continental frigate, by rank, will command the fleet destined to *Penobscot*, to dispossess the enemy there, in conjunction with the militia and train detached for that purpose; and that the commanders of the naval and land forces may harmonise in every stage of their operation, to compleat the destruction of the enemy of the United States, at *Penobscot*: We herewith inclose you a copy of instructions to General *Lovell*, and have the fullest assurance you will give the Commander of the *Warren* such instructions as will tend most cordially to unite the land and naval powers on that expedition.

In the name and behalf of the Council,
I am, Gentlemen,
Your most obedient servant,

Hon. NAVY-BOARD.   J. POWELL, President.

[*The foregoing Letter should have been inserted in the fifteenth page.*]

Council's Letter to the Hon. Meshech Weare, *Esq. President of the State of* New-Hampshire, *dated* July 9, 1779.

SIR,

THE Council did not receive your letter dated the 6th instant, 'till this day, at three o'clock, P. M. or should have sent you an answer by the post. I am directed to inform you that the fleet destined for *Penobscot*, will sail on Sunday next, from *Nantasket*.

The place of rendezvous is the town of *Townsend*, in the county of *Lincoln*. We therefore must request that you would issue your orders to the commander of the *Hampden*, to sail at that time and join the fleet, and pursue such orders as he may receive from *Dudley Saltonstall*, Esq.; commander of the ship *Warren*, who has the command of the fleet; and in case he should not meet the fleet as they pass your harbour that he proceed immediately to *Townsend*, and from thence to proceed with them to *Penobscot*, and co-operate with the rest of the fleet in the expedition against the enemy who are invading the eastern parts of this State: We rely much upon the assistance of this ship.

In the name and behalf of the Council,
I am with esteem,
Your most humble servant,
J. POWELL, President.

Hon. *Meshech Weare*, Esq.

Council's Letter to Colonels Orne *and* Lee, *dated* July 11, 1779.

GENTLEMEN,

THERE are wanted in order to equip the ship *General Putnam*, *Daniel Waters*, commander, on the expedition to *Penobscot*, not less than sixty seamen; the Board therefore earnestly request your exertions and influence immediately to procure the men before-mentioned for the ship *General Putnam*. As you were appointed by the General Court a committee for the purpose of manning such vessels as might be destined upon this expedition, it lays with you to give them such encouragement as you think proper. It is of great importance that the fleet should sail immediately; you will therefore lose no time in executing this business. Least you should fail of procuring the men by inlistment, we have furnished you with a warrant and instructions directed to the Sheriff of the county of *Essex*, or his Deputy, or any Constable, to impress the men for the purpose aforesaid, which you will deliver if you judge it necessary, and shall depend upon your affording your assistance and advice to the civil officer upon this occasion, if the measure should be found necessary; as this ship is impressed specially for this service, you may assure the men they shall be released from the service as soon as the expedition is over. Any money you may advance upon this occasion you will be repaid by the committee employed in this town for a similar purpose. The Council have ordered Capt. *Waters* to sail for *Marblehead*, the first wind; you will deliver what men you may procure by inlistment or impress, to him; or, in case he should not arrive at *Marblehead* seasonably, you will send them to this town, by some safe conveyance.

In the name and behalf of Council,

I am, Gentlemen, &c.

J. POWELL, President.

Colonels *Orne* and *Lee*.

Council's Letter to Elias Hasket Derby, *Esq; dated* July 11, 1779.

SIR,

I AM directed by the Board to desire that you would immediately inform the owners of the ships *Hunter, Hector* and *Black Prince*, that it is the expectation of the Board, that they order their respective captains to proceed with their vessels immediately to *Nantasket* harbour, there to join the fleet under the command of *Dudley Saltonstall*, Esq; and proceed with them on the expedition to *Penobscot*; and in case you cannot readily meet with the owners of the ships before-mentioned, you will communicate these orders to the captains.

In the name and behalf of Council,

I am your humble servant,

J. POWELL, President.

Elias H. Derby, Esq;

Council's Letter to the Navy-Board, dated July 12, 1779.
GENTLEMEN,

THE Council Board having given orders that the ships in the service of this State, and employed in the present expedition to *Penobscot*, proceed to sea upon the signal given from the Continental frigate *Warren*; you are requested to give order to the commander of the said frigate, and other ships under your direction to proceed to the place of rendezvous already agreed to.

In the name and behalf of Council,

J. POWELL, President.

Hon. NAVY-BOARD.

Letter from the Hon. Meshech Weare, *Esq.; President of the honorable Council of the State of* New Hampshire, *to the Hon.* Jeremiah Powell, *Esq; dated* Hampton-Falls, July 6, 1779.

SIR,

I AM honored with the receipt of your favor of the 29th ult. relative to the expedition forming against our enemies at *Penobscot*, which appears to be absolutely necessary, and to be forwarded with all possible expedition.

The General Assembly of this State had adjourned the week before I received your favor, that it could not be laid before them, nor such measures be taken as might have been had they been sitting.

The Committee of Safety for the State, who transact such matters as are of necessity in the recess of the General Court, have agreed to fit out an armed vessel, the *Hamden*, of twenty-two guns, to join in the expedition as speedily as possible, which I expect will be ready to sail in three or four days.

Should be glad to hear by the return of the post, when your fleet are to sail; or any other intelligence you may think proper to communicate. I am with much esteem and respect,

Your obedient humble servant,

MESHECH WEARE.

Hon. *Jeremiah Powell*, Esq;

Council's Letter to the Navy-Board, dated July 14, 1779.

GENTLEMEN,

THIS Board being duly informed by the Board of War, that the ships and vessels in service of this State on the expedition to *Penobscot*, are ready to proceed to sea upon the proper signals being given from the frigate *Warren*; you are requested to give the necessary order to Capt. *Saltonstall*, as soon as may be.

In the name and behalf of the Council,

Your most humble servant,

J. POWELL; President.

Hon. NAVY-BOARD.

Council's Letter to General Lovell, *dated* July 23, 1779.

SIR,

INCLOSED you have the copy of a deposition taken yesterday before a Committee of Council. The deponent's character is not known to the Board. It is the expectation of the Council that you improve intelligence of this nature and importance to the best purpose; and that you will push your operations with all possible vigor and dispatch, and accomplish the business of the expedition before any reinforcement can get to the enemy at *Penobscot*. It is also reported here, and believed by many, that a forty-gun ship and the *Delaware* frigate, sailed from *Sandy-Hook* on the 16th current, and stood to the Eastward; their destination was not known. You will dispatch the packet as soon as may be, the Council being very desirous to know the situation of the army under your command.

In the name and by order of the Council,

I am, Sir, your humble servant,

J. POWELL, President.

Brigadier-General LOVELL.

Council's Letter to Brigadier-General Lovell, *dated* August 6, 1779.

SIR,

THE Council not having received any intelligence of the state of the army under your command since your departure from *Boston*, are apprehensive that it must have been unluckily intercepted; they have therefore ordered the dispatch of an express to you for the purpose of being informed from you with the utmost precision, of your situation and circumstances; the information to be forwarded to this Board without delay. There is no news of the movements of the enemy that may be depended upon. You are fully sensible of the necessity of compleating the design of this expedition with all that speed as well as prudence and discretion which characterizes you as an officer, vested with so important a command.

In the name and behalf of the Council,

I am, Sir, your humble servant,

J. POWELL, President.

Brigadier-General LOVELL.

Council's Letter to General Gates, *dated* August 8, 1779.

SIR,

THE Hon. Mr. *Adams* will communicate to you two letters this Board have received from General *Lovell*, by which you will learn the situation of our army and navy at *Penobscot*, and points out the necessity of his being immediately reinforced with at least four hundred Continental troops, in order effectually and speedily to subdue the enemy there. We must therefore earnestly request your aid and assistance upon this important occasion. We need not enlarge upon this subject, as Mr. *Adams* will give you all the necessary information, and can fully point out to you the fatal consequences that must ensue if this expedition to the Eastward should prove abortive for want of a few Continental troops. We doubt not of your readiness to do every thing in your power to promote the safety and interest of this State, as well as of the United States in general. We have furnished Mr. *Adams* with an order upon Brigadier *Godfrey*, to furnish you with as many militia men out of his brigade, as you may supply us with upon this occasion.

In the name and behalf of the Council,
I am with respect,
Your humble servant,
J. POWELL, President.

General GATES.

Council's Letter to Meshech Weare, *Esq; dated* August 8, 1779.

SIR,

IT appearing by a representation made by Brigadier General *Lovell*, at *Penobscot*, that it is of importance that the brave men under his command should be reinforced with a number of troops well acquainted with military discipline and the art of war, the Council of this State have endeavored to effect that purpose, in which they have pleasing prospects of success, by calling upon several independent and other well disciplined companies in this and the neighbouring towns, to turn out and join the General in his present expedition.

The Council have therefore directed me to give you this notice, that you might use your most strenuous endeavours to co-operate with us in supplying the General with as many men of the above description as you can furnish, and the exigencies of the case in question may require. The Council rest assured from your known zeal, and that of your State, for the public cause, that every thing in your power will be done to effect so interesting a purpose. You must be sensible that the whole efficacy depends on the greatest dispatch and expedition.   In the name and behalf of Council,

J. POWELL, President.

Hon. MESHECH WEARE, Esq;

Council's Letter to the Hon. Enoch Freeman *or* Samuel Freeman, Esq'rs *dated* August 10, 1779.

SIR,

IT is the desire of the Council, that you will procure an express and immediately send him forward (either by land or water as will be most expeditious) to Brigadier-General *Lovell*, with the enclosed letter from this Board, which is to inform the General that a reinforcement is now on their way to him.

In the name and behalf of Council,
I am your humble servant,
J. POWELL, President.

Enoch Freeman or *Samuel Freeman*, Esq'rs.

Council's Letter to General Lovell, *dated* August 10, 1779.

SIR,

THE Council received your letters of the 30th ultimo, have attentively considered the contents, congratulate you on the successes that have attended you since your arrival at *Penobscot*. The Council have lost no time in procuring a reinforcement to the army under your command, and on application made to Major-General *Gates* for that purpose, they this moment by express received advice from *Providence*, that the General had ordered Col. *Jackson's* regiment, consisting of four hundred men to march to your assistance, and that the detachment would be in town to-morrow: You will rest assured, Sir, that no time will be lost or exertion omitted by the Council to forward the detachment with the greatest expedition. The Council thought it of importance that you should have the earliest notice of this event, and have accordingly forwarded this letter by express; have only time to add that the other matters contained in your letters will be duly attended to, of which you will have further advice in our next. Wishing you prosperity and success,

I am, in behalf of Coucil,
Your humble servant,
J. POWELL, President.

General *Lovell*.

198

Council's Letter to Selectmen and Commanders of Independent Companies in *Salem* and *Marblehead, dated* August 10, 1779.

GENTLEMEN,

ON the 8th instant the Council addressed you on the subject of sending a number of your troops, well acquainted with military movements, to the assistance of General *Lovell,* at *Penobscot;* but as the Council have received no answer, they are apprehensive that some accident must have taken place and prevent the express reaching you. The bearer came on purpose to know the fate of the Council's application, and to request you would immediately return the express with an exact account of the number of troops that we are to expect on this pressing occasion, of this you will not fail. In the name and behalf of the Council,

J. POWELL, President.

The Gentlemen Selectmen and Companies Independent and Volunteers.

Council's Letter to General Lovell, *dated* August 11, 1779.

SIR,

WE yesterday sent you an account by express, that General *Gates* had ordered Col. *Henry Jackson's* regiment, consisting of between three and four hundred men, to reinforce you; they are expected in town to-morrow noon, and may probably sail from hence on Friday or Saturday; as they will go with a small convoy, we shall direct them to keep in shore, which will somewhat retard their progress; but we judge it nevertheless a prudent course for their greater safety. We have just now received a letter from General *Washington,* inclosing a copy of a letter from an officer at *Newark* to Lord *Stirling,* which was forwarded to General *Washington,* copies of which you have inclosed: We forwarded them to you from hence by land to *Falmouth,* and from thence both by land and water, for the greater security, and that you may as soon as possible be acquainted with their contents, and direct your movements accordingly. The Council believes the ships and troops mentioned in the inclosed papers are really intended to reinforce your enemy. We would advise you and the naval commander, if 'tis thought any way practicable, to collect as great a force as possible from the fleet, and make an attack upon the enemy's strong hold without delay; whether the destruction or capture of their ships should be first attempted, you will consider and determine; if neither can be attempted with any probability of success, we advise you to re-embark and retreat as quick as possible to some more secure post, where you may cover the Eastern country from the ravages of the enemy, should they attempt to ravage it; perhaps *Townsend* may be a proper post. You will give us the earliest intelligence of your movements, and wait our further orders. Your situation is very critical; something must be hazarded, and speedily too; delay may operate to your destruction. You are not to delay your operations in expectation of any assistance from Col. *Jackson's* regiment; but to take your measures with your present force. 'Tis probable the Council will direct Col. *Jackson's* regiment to touch in at *Townsend*, and there learn your state and condition before he proceeds to join you.

In the name and behalf of the Council,
I am your most humble servant,
J. POWELL, President.

General *Lovell*.

Council's Letter to General Lovell, *dated* August 12, 1779.

SIR,

THIS morning your letter of the 6th instant, by Major *Braddish*, was laid before Council with the inclosures, which we have communicated to the Navy-Board. In consequence of which the Navy-Board have by this opportunity sent positive instructions to Capt. *Saltonstall*, a copy of which is here inclosed. By this you will clearly see the opinion and order of the Navy-Board, in which opinion the Council are in sentiment.

In the name and behalf of Council,
I am your humble servant,
J. POWELL, President.

General *Lovell*.

Navy-Board's Letter to Commodore Saltonstall, *dated* August 12, 1779.

SIR,

MAJOR *Braddish* this morning arrived with dispatches from General *Lovell* to the honorable Council. We don't find that he has brought any for us; the Council, however, have obliged us with a communication of General *Lovell's* letter, and the papers inclosed; among which we find the result of a Council of War on board the *Warren, August*, 1779. We have for sometime been at a loss to know why the enemy's ships have not been attacked, nor does the result of this Council give us any satisfaction on that head; it is agreed on all hands that they are at all times in your power. If, therefore, your own security, or the more advantageous operations of the army did not require it, why should any business be delayed to another day, that may as well be done this? Our apprehensions of your danger have ever been from a reinforcement to the enemy; you can't expect to remain much longer without one. Whatever, therefore, is to be done, should be done immediately, both to prevent advantages to the enemy, and delays if you are obliged to retreat. As we presume you would avoid having these ships in your rear while a reinforcement appears in front, or the necessity of leaving them behind when you retire yourself; with these sentiments, we think it our duty to direct you to attack and take or destroy them without delay, in doing which no time is to be lost, as a reinforcement are probably on their passage at this time. It is therefore our orders that as soon as you receive this you take the most effectual measures for the capture or destruction of the enemy's ships, and with the greatest dispatch the nature and situation of things will admit of.

We are your friends and servants,
W. VERNON.
J. WARREN.

Commodore *Saltonstall.*
[COPY.]

Proceedings of a Committee of the General Assembly, respecting the Failure of the Penobscot *expedition, dated* October 7, 1779.

THE Committee of both Houses appointed to enquire into the reasons of the failure of the late *Penobscot* expedition, have, after giving due notice to the Commanders by land and sea and cited such persons as the Committee judged most likely to give the best account of the reasons of the failure aforesaid, proceeded to enquire into the causes of said failure. General *Lovell's* narrative of his procedure, with the Councils of War by land and by sea, and the depositions of the several witnesses delivered in on this enquiry accompanying this report, and the opinion of your Committee upon the aforesaid subject will appear as follows:

1st QUESTION. Is it the opinion of this Committee that they have made sufficient enquiry into the causes of the failure of the late expedition to *Penobscot*?

ANSWER, *unanimously*,—Yes.

2d QUESTION. What appears to be the principal reason of the failure?

ANSWER, *unanimously*,—Want of proper spirit and energy on the part of the Commodore.

3d QUESTION. Was General *Lovell* culpable in not storming the enemy's principal fort according to the requirement of the Commodore and Naval-Council, who insisted upon that as the condition of our ships attacking the enemy's ships, when at the same time the Commodore informed him, that in case of such an attack he must call the marines on board their ships. The last was not made a part of the condition by the Naval-Council?

ANSWER, *unanimously*,—No.

4th QUESTION. What, in the opinion of this Committee, was the occasion of the total destruction of our fleet?

ANSWER. Principally the Commodore's not exerting himself at all at the time of the retreat, in opposing the enemy's foremost ships in pursuit.

5th QUESTION. Does it appear that General *Lovell*, thoughout the expedition and the retreat, acted with proper courage and spirit?

ANSWER, *unanimously*—Yes; and it is the opinion of the Committee had he been furnished with all the men ordered for the service, or been properly supported by the Commodore, he would probably have reduced the enemy.

6th QUESTION. Does it appear that the Commodore discouraged any enterprizes or offensive measures on the part of our fleet?

ANSWER, *unanimously*—Yes; and though he always had a majority of the Naval-Council against offensive operations, which majority was mostly made up of the commanders of private armed vessels, yet he repeatedly said, it was matter of favor that he called any Councils, and when he had taken their advice he should follow his own opinion.

As the Naval Commanders in the service of the State are particularly amenable to the Government, the Committee think it their duty to say, that each and every of them behaved like brave and experienced good officers, throughout the whole of the expedition.

7th QUESTION. What was the conduct of Brigadier *Wadsworth*, during his command?

ANSWER. Brigadier *Wadsworth* (the second in command) throughout the whole expedition, during the retreat, and after, 'till ordered to return to *Boston*, conducted with great activity, courage, coolness and prudence.

The Committee find the number of men ordered to be detached for this service were deficient nearly one third. Whether the shameful neglect is chargeable upon the Brigadiers, Colonels, or other officers, whose particular duty it might have been to have faithfully executed the orders of the General Assembly, they cannot ascertain.

ARTEMAS WARD, per order.

P R E S E N T.

General WARD, General TITCOMB,
Mr. DANA, General FARLEY,
General DANIELSON, Major OSGOOD.
Boston, October 7, 1779.

THE foregoing Papers are true Copies from the Originals, as on File in the Secretary's Office.

Attest. JOHN AVERY, D. Secretary.